For Robin Miller,

THE FLATPACK
BOMBERS

With congratulations on
buying the first signed
copy of the first edition
of the Flatpack Bombers.

Ian Gardiner

4 June 2009

THE FLATPACK BOMBERS

BOMBERS

The Royal Navy and the 'Zeppelin Menace'

Ian Gardiner

Pen & Sword
AVIATION

First published in Great Britain in 2009 by
PEN & SWORD MILITARY
An imprint of
Pen & Sword Books Ltd
47 Church Street
Barnsley
South Yorkshire
S70 2AS

ISBN 978 1 84884 071 3

A CIP catalogue record for this book is
available from the British Library

Printed and bound in England
By CPI

Pen & Sword Books Ltd incorporates the Imprints of Pen & Sword Aviation,
Pen & Sword Family History, Pen & Sword Maritime, Pen & Sword Military,
Wharncliffe Local History, Pen & Sword Select, Pen & Sword Military Classics,
Leo Cooper, Remember When, Seaforth Publishing and Frontline Publishing

For a complete list of Pen & Sword titles please contact
PEN & SWORD BOOKS LIMITED
47 Church Street, Barnsley, South Yorkshire, S70 2AS, England
E-mail: enquiries@pen-and-sword.co.uk
Website: www.pen-and-sword.co.uk

*In salute to the memory and example of the men of the
Royal Naval Air Service of the Royal Navy,
and of the Naval Airship Division
of the Imperial German Navy 1912–1918*

Contents

Maps

Foreword

This book is one that can be read and savoured at two very different levels. First of all, as a set of tales of human endeavour and extraordinary derring-do, *The Flatpack Bombers* will be hard to beat, not least because of the author's obvious empathy with the heroic men whose exploits he recounts. Given his own background and experience, this is perhaps not too surprising and it makes for a highly enjoyable read.

The second and perhaps rather more serious level of analysis is to look at the experience of *The Flatpack Bombers* as an example of the way in which military men introduce new technology into the business of war and then exploit it operationally. For many years, it was fashionable to say that senior military figures have a natural proclivity to prepare to fight the last war rather than the next one, and that part and parcel of the reason for this is an innate conservatism that makes them deeply resistant to the unsettling effects of new technology. The nineteenth-century Royal Navy, for example, has been widely condemned for its attitude to the introduction of steam propulsion, torpedoes and submarines. In the twentieth century, one of the most common criticisms was that senior officers just could not grasp the revolutionary potential of aircraft at sea, delayed it for as long as they unreasonably could, and accordingly suffered such disasters as the sinking of the *Prince of Wales* and the *Repulse* by Japanese aircraft in December 1941.

The argument goes like this. Military men are at their most impressionable at an early stage in their career when they are trying to make sense of the complicated and unfamiliar world which they have just entered. This is a difficult process and, as a result, the hard-won and emerging conclusions will often prove hard to shake off. Technology then develops faster than their impressions and conclusions do, and so there is a widening gap between technical reality and the perceptions of it that senior military men will often have.

This kind of argument has the merit of great simplicity but of little else. The most obvious flaw in it is that the senior military men on the other side of the hill (in this case the Japanese High Command behind the attack on Malaya in 1941) somehow didn't seem to suffer from this disease, or at least not at the same time. Clearly some people are prone to this, and some people aren't. Accepting this caveat immediately gets us away from simplistic and blanket condemnations into the much more useful and nuanced business of looking at the more detailed 'hows' and 'whys' that explain the way in which new technology gets taken into the business of war – what the problems are and the process is. The more we go into particular case studies of this, the more we tend to realise that there are not just two but many sides of the matter to consider.

Nowadays, historians take a much more sympathetic and understanding view of the nineteenth-century Royal Navy than they did, pointing out that given their straitened financial circumstances and the huge uncertainties of the maritime technology of the time, British admirals in fact kept up with the hunt to a remarkable degree, and were indeed at the forefront of such developments as the introduction of submarines, mines, radio-telephony, and so on. Their problem was, and indeed for their successors remains, that the particular future of technology in any given sphere was, and is, very hard to call in advance and, for the safety of their country and the lives of their people, they simply cannot afford to get it radically wrong. For this reason, there is a natural, understandable and indeed entirely valid tendency to make haste slowly until the dust begins to settle sufficiently for irreversible investments to be made safely.

This, of course, conflicts with the image that people often have of technological advance – namely that someone comes up with a bright idea that immediately transforms the situation, perhaps as the atom bombs of August 1945 seemed to do. In fact this is rarely the way things happen. Usually technological innovation comes about not so much through a single revolutionary jump as a series of minor advances turning into a kind of evolutionary slither. Bright and sometimes adventurous people constantly advance the cause by having and implementing good ideas that improve their capabilities by just a bit – they seek practical solutions to the countless succession of little technical problems that they encounter, while the bright and adventurous people on the other side seek to counter or outdo their achievements in just the same way. This is a rather different and indeed rather more convincing vision of technical change than the notion of the dramatic impact of supposedly 'transformational' technology that was so common in the 1990s.

The Flatpack Bombers documents all this in an area of military advance that is still relatively unstudied. This is surprising for not only are the early exploits of naval aviation nearly a hundred years ago a fascinating and still relevant example of the way in which new technology is introduced into the business of war, but they were also the first stirrings of strategic bombing – a form of military action that was later to become one of the defining characteristics of war in the twentieth, and indeed the twenty-first century. For all these reasons, this enjoyable and important book is highly recommended.

Professor Geoffrey Till, Director,

Corbett Centre for Maritime Policy Studies, King's College, London.

Acknowledgements

It seems to me that whatever you write about as a historian, there is always someone somewhere who knows something more about your subject than you do. For this book, I have been most fortunate in being able to rely heavily upon a number of people much more experienced, and infinitely more eminent than I, to guide me and ensure that my musings remained within what is historically likely or possible. Chief among these illustrious allies has been Professor Eric Grove of Salford University. Professor Grove gave most freely of his time and very considerable energy. Without the benefit of his knowledge and expertise, the book would have been a lesser and much more inaccurate work. I am especially grateful to him.

Major General Julian Thompson, ever supportive and encouraging, very kindly did a sanity check on an early draft and ensured that my assertions about the Royal Navy of 1914 were not too far out of station. Professor Geoffrey Best helpfully gave me some valuable compass bearings to put me on the trail of the origins of strategic bombing.

I am also greatly indebted to Mr Iain MacKenzie of the Admiralty Library in Portsmouth Naval Base who, at the very inception of this project, gave most generously of his time and encyclopaedic knowledge to set me off on the right track. No historian could have been given a better leg up than the papers he researched, copied and sent to me, even before the first words appeared on my computer.

A decent foreword gives a book a context. If the author is lucky, and he persuades the right man to write it, it also brings a magisterial gravity that the author himself has no chance of generating by his own pen. I am most grateful to Professor Geoffrey Till, Director of the Corbett Centre for Maritime Policy Studies, King's College, London for openhandedly and expertly providing that very service.

Without the critical and expert help of Herr Jürgen Bleibler, Archivist of the Zeppelin Museum in Friedrichshafen, this book would have been much the poorer. His knowledge of these remarkable airships is extraordinary and he added an extra dimension, bringing detail, depth, accuracy and balance that I could never have achieved without his enthusiastic, generous and most valuable contribution.

The Library of the Joint Services Command and Staff College has been an essential source of books and journals. The staff there, led by Mr Chris Hobson, himself a notable author on aviation subjects, have been patient, kind and professional, and I could not have done without them. Mr Hobson also did me the most valuable service of reading the typescript and checking for nonsense at an early stage.

Mr Jeremy Jamieson kindly lent me his grandfather, Murray Sueter's, book, *Airmen and Noahs*, and provided a unique insight into that remarkable man who was pivotal to the nascent Royal Naval Air Service. I am also grateful to Dr Timm Gudehus of Hamburg who showed me the memoirs of his grandfather, H.C. Gustav Gudehus, who was the shipbroker who arranged the purchase and conversion of the German passenger ship *Lahn* to the Russian captive balloon carrier *Russ*. Mr Harry Smee also gave me some valuable information about his grandfather, Lieutenant Frank Brock, who assisted in the planning and execution of the Friedrichshafen raid. Some early aero engines had a pronounced gyroscopic effect which induced distinctive flight characteristics in the aircraft they powered. I thank Mr James Mattocks and Mr Philip Stephens for their assistance in teasing out just what those characteristics were.

The staffs of the Archive of the Luftschiffbau Zeppelin GmbH in Friedrichshafen, the National Archive at Kew, the Fleet Air Arm Museum at Yeovilton, the Imperial War Museum in London, the Admiralty Library in Portsmouth Naval Base and the College Library at Royal Air Force Cranwell could not have been more helpful. All of these also kindly assisted with the provision of photographs which are attributed appropriately on the plates.

Every author has intimates who, if he or she is lucky, help and support his or her efforts in a thousand different ways. I am indeed fortunate in this regard. My wife Louise took meticulous care in exorcising my grammatical and stylistic waywardness, and our children Catriona and Angus, not only read the typescript and applied their own sanity checks, but above all were patient and kind with me when I banged on about aircraft and airships a little more than perhaps their own natural interest in the subject warranted. And indeed, I owe the title of the book itself to Catriona's imagination.

Every author needs a publisher, and I am most grateful to Henry Wilson and Pen & Sword for taking me on for a second time. My editor, Bobby Gainher, smoothed the process from my computer to the final article with speed, style and understanding.

It was Flight Lieutenant John Babington's account of his part in the Friedrichshafen Raid which sparked my intention to write this book. I am therefore especially grateful to his daughter, Mrs Penelope Willis, for showing me that account and for letting me use it. She and her late husband Tony, as well as offering much warm friendship over the past thirty-five years, were a valued source of encouragement and enthusiasm for the book. I am also indebted to the late Dr Norman Lyne who edited John Babington's typescript for his own book on the subject, a work which sadly never saw the light of day.

Finally, notwithstanding the proofreading, sanity checks and lie detector service that all the above have generously and skilfully provided, any nonsense and all cock-ups remain on my slop chit.

Introduction

History has its well worn paths. One might suppose that so much has been said about the First World War that there isn't much more to say. But so many people took part, and the diversity of activities was so great over its four and a quarter years' duration, that one can always find some unbeaten grass off the wide, main tracks which, when explored, reveals yet another fascinating story. Most of these stories are simply very small pieces in the jigsaw, which when found, do not substantially change our understanding of the bigger picture. This one, I think, is a little more than that.

The 1914 naval air raids on Düsseldorf, Friedrichshafen and Cuxhaven have been written about before, and this book makes no new claims upon our understanding of history. But so far as I am aware, no one has drawn together so many of their threads into one skein. It is also a question of emphasis. Possession of the Zeppelin gave Germany potential strategic supremacy in the air in 1914 and 1915. I do wonder whether that fact has always been accorded its due importance. It certainly exercised the minds of the British leaders of the day and was the reason why the British government originally formed the Royal Flying Corps – a joint Army-Navy organisation and the world's first prototype air force.

Given the preoccupation of the Military Wing of the new Royal Flying Corps with directly supporting the Army, it was left to the Naval Wing to solve the Zeppelin problem. British victory in the pre-war naval armaments race was in danger of being negated by the Zeppelin's ability to spy at sea, and Britain's hitherto inviolate island was about to have its moat crossed by behemoths the size of ocean liners, with bomb payloads which still match those of today's bombers nine decades later. And there was no means of shooting them down! In other words, Germany enjoyed potential strategic air supremacy. The only chance of countering the Zeppelins was to destroy them on the ground. But their bases were hundreds of miles from the sea, deep in Germany.

In 1914, the striking range of even the most powerful navy in the world was limited by the maximum distance to which it could fire its guns. In the case of the Royal Navy that was 24,300 yards – supposing one could see what one was shooting at. In theory this was extended to 30,000 yards when HMS *Furious* with her single, monstrous, 18-inch gun appeared in 1917. Powerful though these guns were, they were not effective against aircraft or airships. Conventional methods of dealing with Zeppelins offered no answers. Winston Churchill, as the political head of the Royal Navy, therefore resorted to unconventional means of destroying them. This meant somehow extending the reach of naval power projection hundreds of miles beyond the range of naval guns. The solution took the form of the naval air raids on Düsseldorf, Friedrichshafen and, using seaplane carriers, of striking at Cuxhaven – the first strategic bombing raids in history.

So the Zeppelin airship was a catalyst which helped to shape many modern navies because the evolution of the modern aircraft carrier owes much to these early attempts to counter the Zeppelin. And as incidental by-products of these raids, the Royal Navy sired the armoured car and the tank, and pioneered co-operation between air and armoured land forces – all in the first three months of the First World War. And who would have guessed that the first strategic bombing raid ever was carried out by Royal Marines? Such are the rewards to be found in the long grass, off the beaten track of history.

Winston Churchill's fingerprints are all over this story. His central role in the Second World War sometimes throws into shadow the key part he played in the earlier conflict. His character and enthusiasms coincided neatly with the rapid evolution of the Naval Wing of the Royal Flying Corps into an autonomous Royal Naval Air Service. During the few years of its existence, the Royal Naval Air Service was a very special organisation, occupying a bureaucratic no man's land outside the mainstream Admiralty, and with little integration with the other half of the Royal Flying Corps. The new dimension of the air attracted adventurous spirits of diverse talents and backgrounds to whom fast cars and flying offered liberation from the formal social flummery of Edwardian Britain. With flying – even more so with flying at sea – you were as good as your last mistake; or someone else's mistake. And your first mistake could well be your last one. No doubt Churchill's influence was part of it. For him, one life was simply not enough. He revelled in living through the lives of young men who demonstrated the same zest for innovation, excitement and danger that he had, and were doing things which, if he had been younger, he would certainly have done himself. Under his aegis, all these came together in a most vital and fecund flourish.

The Royal Naval Air Service with its armoured vehicles, motorcyclist machine gunners, armoured artillery trains, anti-aircraft batteries and tank development team was more of a private army than the simple air wing of the Navy and, when Churchill resigned from the Admiralty in 1915, some of the momentum was undoubtedly lost.

Officers in the Royal Naval Air Service may have worn four different styles of rank during their service. When they came from the mainstream

Royal Navy, they started with naval or Royal Marines rank and assumed Royal Naval Air Service rank. When the Royal Air Force was formed in 1918 out of the Royal Flying Corps and the Royal Naval Air Service, everybody took a military rank until, in 1919, the Royal Air Force ranks that we use today were instituted. There was not a direct equivalence between Royal Naval Air Service and naval ranks. Royal Naval Air Service rank has been used where appropriate throughout this book.

All the players in this story have long been gathered to their fathers but, thirty years ago, I met John Babington not long before he died. At the time, I was a young and very junior Royal Marines officer, while he was a very senior and long-retired Royal Air Force officer. We enjoyed the sort of conversation one might expect to pass between two such men: agreeable enough, but neither knowing sufficient about the other's world to ask intelligent questions, or to elicit interesting answers.

I wish that I had known then what I know now. When his daughter, Mrs Penelope Willis, recently let me see his personal account of the Friedrichshafen Raid, I knew I had found the subject of my second book. As soon as I read the account, I wanted to write about it. The passion necessary for a second opus had been ignited. The more I studied and the more I wrote, the more I realised that here was a story which, although it can be traced in fragments and in outline, has never been set out in full in one piece. Intrinsically it deserves it. But it deserves further treatment because of its place in the genesis of the many strategic bombing raids that have taken place since, and perhaps because of what it might conceivably still teach us about other raids in future.

The Friedrichshafen Raid, the Düsseldorf Raids which preceded it, and the Cuxhaven Raid which followed it were the first strategic bombing raids in history. I have taken the word 'strategic' in this context simply to mean actions beyond the immediate battlefield intended to affect the enemy's ability to fight, rather than action between forces already engaged or committed to the battlefield.

I have drawn on various sources, including some accounts of those who took part, but written many years after the events described. The human memory is a notoriously unreliable database and, notwithstanding the authoritative nature of such a first-hand account, where it has conflicted with a contemporary record, I have tended to rely upon the latter. In addition, no two people will give precisely the same account of any one event. Reconciling two views of the same event is not always easy. Where two stories differ beyond reconciliation, I have given both.

This isn't intended to be a 'nuts and bolts' book – although there is a bit of that. Neither does it seek to set out the grand philosophical sweep of history, although there is some attempt at interpretation without which the

3

bare facts are pretty sterile. Above all, it tries to tell a story. History is a story – the story so far. The story of our forebears is a ripping, gripping, rollercoaster of a yarn, far better than any fiction could ever be.

So, as well as being an attempt at describing and interpreting history, this book seeks to paint a vivid picture of what it must have been like to fly at the dawn of the age of aviation. A great deal has been written about the Army's Royal Flying Corps, and the truths, myths and legends of the air war in France that was fought with so much gallantry on both sides, are deeply ingrained in our imaginations. Albert Ball, James McCudden, Manfred von Richthofen, Oswald Boelke and Max Immelmann are not about to fade from popular memory. Less well known is the story of the Royal Naval Air Service, although it too made important contributions to the Western Front air war. The remarkably wide-ranging operations of its aircrew over land and sea made them, rather than their khaki-clad brethren, the true precursors of their successors in the Royal Air Force in the application of 'air power'. Not for nothing do Royal Air Force officers, albeit usually unknowingly, to this day wear the Royal Naval Air Service cap badge.

Nevertheless, only *aficionados* have heard of Charles Samson, Charles Collet, Eugene Gerrard, Reggie Marix, Sidney Sippe, Spenser Grey, John Babington or Edward Briggs. Even fewer still know the names of the ten men who flew on the first carrier air strike in history – or that the spy thriller writer and Irish nationalist, Erskine Childers, was among their number. And yet in the first few months of the war, on virtually every operation, these men and their colleagues were pushing the boundaries of flight further than they had ever been pushed before. And every bombing raid in history since, from land or sea, and every aircraft carrier, can trace its pedigree to their endeavours.

Their targets were Zeppelins. The men who crewed these lighter-than-air monsters too were pioneers of the first rank. In their driving ambition to take them higher, further and faster, they can be compared to astronauts of our own day. It is the curse of war that it should pit men of such high calibre and surpassing gallantry against each other. But for historians and for those who read history, it is an uplifting and humbling joy to relive – even if only vicariously – the lives of those who did such splendid things. If I have in even the smallest way helped a reader to share that pleasure, I will be well satisfied.

Ian Ritchie Gardiner
Edinburgh 2009

Chapter 1

Lost in the Air

Flight Commander John Babington of the Royal Naval Air Service cursed the fact that he had no map. Once more he peered desperately into the fading light trying to recognise something of the landscape that he had flown over in bright sunlight in the opposite direction some four hours before. Having spent these hours in an open cockpit at over 4,000 feet in winter, he was bitterly cold. The light was deteriorating, his fuel was low and he would have to land very soon wherever he was. But where was he? He hoped and believed he was over France but he couldn't be sure. It could equally well be neutral Switzerland and to land there would not do. That would mean internment for him and his aeroplane, and he would miss all the prospective action that this war offered. He thought he had crossed the Rhine, but if he hadn't, it could be Germany. The thought of spending the remainder of the war as a prisoner appalled him – and all because he had no map.

He wished he had disobeyed his orders. It was quite plain that the idiots who insisted that he carry no map of France had never flown in an aeroplane, let alone flown 250 miles in one. He had tried to memorise the point where he had crossed the Rhine on the outward journey, and had made a note of the reciprocal course he would have to follow to get home again. But nothing looked quite the same in this light – or from this direction. He checked his compass. It wavered erratically. The weather had been so clear all day that he had been able to navigate to his target by following landmarks on the ground. He had hardly bothered about his compass, or even the map of Germany which he did have.

He wiped the thin film of engine oil from his goggles. Where was the huge hangar at Belfort that he was looking for? One could hardly miss it. He swung right. The country looked too flat. He swung left and then he circled round. All sorts of things which, in the distance, looked as if they might have been the hangar at Belfort, turned out not to be. Now, markedly overdue, and fuel at a minimum, he decided he must land or crash. He concentrated on finding somewhere to land – anywhere to land. There was nothing but small fields and, judging from the trees, there didn't seem to be any wind. Finally he chose the long side of one particular field which sloped decidedly upwards. He landed with a bit of bump, but safely enough. He cut the engine. Suddenly, after fours hours sitting behind his throbbing, fulminating, rotating engine, the silence was stunning.

There was a small hamlet close by. Where was he? Was he in France? If not, he might have to burn the machine. He turned on what remained of the petrol and let it drip. Bitterly cold and extremely stiff, he clambered with difficulty out of the cockpit. He had long since lost any sensation of feeling in his feet. He relieved himself on the grass next to his plane. Stamping around to try and get some blood flowing, he fumbled in his pocket for his lighter just in case he needed to torch his plane. Meanwhile, he lit a welcome cigarette and drew in deeply. No one was in sight. With his pistol in one hand and his lighter in the other, Flight Commander John Babington sat down on the grass to wait. And so ended one of the first strategic air bombing raids in history.

This was November 1914. John Babington and his two comrades, all three of them officers in the Royal Navy with dual rank in the Royal Naval Air Service, had just bombed the Zeppelin construction shed at Friedrichshafen in southern Germany on the northern shore of Lake Constance. The aircraft they were flying were brand-new machines which had been packed into cases in kit form by the manufacturers and shipped to the mounting airfield in France. There, inside an unheated balloon hangar in winter, the planes had been assembled for the first time. When they lifted off from the grass strip on their epoch-making raid, it was the first time these particular aeroplanes had taken to the air.

Strictly speaking, this was not the first strategic bombing raid in history – Lieutenant Charles Collet of the Royal Marine Artillery had claimed that 'first' when he had bombed the Zeppelin shed in Düsseldorf two months earlier. And their brother naval officers, Reginald Marix and Spenser Grey had then gone on to bomb that same Zeppelin shed in Düsseldorf again, and the railway station in Cologne respectively, two weeks later. But these raids had been ad hoc affairs compared to the carefully planned and executed Friedrichshafen raid. In terms of planning, preparation, and aims, the Friedrichshaven Raid was the progenitor of all air raids ever since.

This is the story of those earliest raids. This is the story of why, for a few critical months in 1914 and 1915, the behemoth airships known as Zeppelins struck fear and apprehension into the minds of the British people and their political and military leaders. It is also the story of how the Royal Navy set about countering this threat to its supremacy at sea, and how, in the first few months of the First World War, the Royal Navy, led by Winston Churchill, pioneered strategic bombing and aircraft carriers, and sent its aircraft to strike land targets several hundred miles from the nearest sea – all when flying itself was barely out of its infancy.

Chapter 2

A New Dimension to War

So why was the Royal Navy so concerned with bombing strategic targets several hundred miles from the sea in 1914, a few short months into the First World War?

Traditional naval historians have not been kind to the nineteenth-century Royal Navy. It has been argued that, although the Royal Navy had policed Pax Britannica most effectively and largely unchallenged after 1815, it was afflicted by that disease which can hit any large successful organisation: the sclerosis of success. Every organisation has a corporate memory which, if it is not constantly revitalised, eventually tends to fade and drift away from the central purpose and principles of its business. After so many years of comparative peace, it used to be argued, the Royal Navy's memory of war had subsided into shadow. Certainly, hard sailing there had been aplenty and the anti-piracy and anti-slaving operations, in which the Royal Navy had played the leading part, had exacted a steady toll of lives. Nevertheless, the Navy had forgotten what really happened in conflict – its success in keeping the peace had erased the realities of war from its corporate consciousness. This, together with the Victorians' love of order, and their tendency to control, to regulate, to tidy things up, and the importance of appearances, had produced a crippling culture of mindless obedience and deference to rank. People would obey the last order, however dysfunctional it might appear, until they received the next order. Nobody was encouraged to use his brain, unless one day he became the admiral. It was then assumed that, as if by some process of immaculate conception, he had become all-knowing and the fount of all wisdom. Initiative, discussion, innovation – except from the top – was distinctly discouraged.

Much had changed since Nelson's day in the character of naval officership, it was said, and much of that was for the worse. The essentially practical nature of the profession had been reinforced by technical progress into an almost total fixation with materiel and the Newtonian physical 'laws' which described how the technology worked. The creation of the initial training scheme in the second half of the century in the *Britannia* at

Dartmouth only made the situation worse as the teenage cadets were put through mind-stretching mathematical gymnastics. Late-Victorian naval officers lived in a world of physical laws and calculations. They were technologists rather than tacticians, scientists rather than strategists.

The Nelsonian concept of a 'pell-mell battle', where decisions were taken by commanders on the spot in support of their admiral's intentions, was wholly lost to late-Victorian admirals. They had forgotten that war is the province of the unexpected, the province of chaos. Nelson knew that the man at the top of the organisation was not best placed to decide on every detail down through that organisation. He knew that if he tried to impose a detailed prescribed plan on a dynamic, unforeseeable situation he would fail. He knew that he couldn't rely on communications during a battle and so he didn't even try to communicate. Instead, before the battle, he explained to his captains what it was he wanted, and why. He talked through with them all the possibilities they could think of – all the constraints and the priorities – and then trusted them to get on with it. He invited them into his brain so that they could speak and act for him without the need to consult him. In this way his captains were able to respond appropriately to the fluid circumstances they saw unfolding in front of them without hesitation and delay. He gave them great freedom of action, but they always knew what to do. When the famous 'England expects ...' signal appeared on *Victory*'s yardarm, Collingwood, who was Nelson's second-in-command, before he read it, harrumphed. 'I wish Nelson would stop signalling,' he said. 'We all of us know well enough what to do.' Nelson's only other signal at Trafalgar was: 'Engage the enemy more closely' – get stuck in lads, you know what to do. 'His greatest gift of leadership was to raise his juniors above the need of supervision.'[1] For the late Victorians, the notion that it was the duty of the leader to raise his juniors above the need of supervision would be to turn the natural order of mankind on its head. Such an absurdity would never have occurred to them.

Although Victoria herself had exited the stage thirteen years before, in 1914 the Royal Navy was still a true reflection of Great Britain in the Victorian age. Like Victorian society, the Navy was profoundly hierarchical and everyone knew their place. Promotion from the lower deck to commissioned rank was rare. It was a navy where the patriarchs of the family, the ship captains, were god-like figures who expected and, in the main received, unquestioning obedience. Corporal punishment, which had been abolished in the Army, was still possible in the Navy where a man could be caned on the orders of his captain. Communication was limited to telling people precisely what to do. And they communicated all the time doing just that. Every detail of administration, every change of course of each ship during manoeuvres and during battle, was subject to the decision of a superior. It is indicative that the Brahmins, the Heaven-born, of all the officer specialisations were the signals officers – the communicators – and the best brains, or at least the most self-important brains, of the Navy were bent on producing newer, better ways of passing information and signalling to each other. Henry Jackson, later to be First Sea Lord, was as much a pioneer of wireless telegraphy as Marconi. Because good communications were now technically possible, commanders used them all the time and they came to rely upon them. But in truth they had become obsessed with the process rather than the product.

This description has long been the received historical view of the Victorian Royal Navy. And yet how was it that this 'drowsy, inefficient, moth-eaten organisation'[2] succeeded in embracing with both arms the new dimension of conflict portended by the Wright brothers in 1903? How was it that the Royal Navy led the world in understanding and turning into reality the potential that aircraft offered them? And how was it that the Royal Navy went to war in 1914 with the largest, most developed and promising naval air capability of all the belligerents?

While it cannot be denied that the portrait described above is a recognisable likeness, a new generation of historians of the Royal Navy has painted a more balanced picture.[3] The Royal Navy of the nineteenth century has now emerged as, in some ways, a remarkably progressive organisation, adopting each piece of revolutionary new technology almost as soon as it presented itself – and with a speed of procurement that throws into the shade the arthritic procurement practices of today. Paddle steamers, shell-firing guns, screw propellers, rifled artillery, armour plate, iron construction, automobile torpedoes, compound engines, quick-firing guns – all these conspired to wreak repeated technological revolutions; revolutions to which the Admiralty had to adjust in order to maintain the war-fighting capacity that was always the bottom line of naval policy.

Moreover, the view we have of the long, leisurely Edwardian garden party through our sepia-tinted photographs is indeed deceptive. By the beginning of the First World War, the Royal Navy had been through, and had managed more or less successfully, a period of bewildering change – in spite of the lack of a professional staff. We in the computerised early twenty-first century may feel that nothing before ever altered so much and so rapidly as it has done in our own lifetime. But a man who joined the Royal Navy in, say 1890, and was still serving in 1914 – and there were many such men – would have lived through a period of remarkable change, easily the match of anything outside of wartime that we might have experienced in the subsequent century.

For instance, our man who joined the Navy in 1890 would have served with sailors who had manned a navy dominated by sailing ships, and who no doubt regaled him with the virtues of the days when men were real sailors. Nevertheless, when he joined in 1890, all ships were powered by coal. By 1914, the transformation to oil-fired boilers was well under way. Radio, the turbine engine, the torpedo, larger and larger calibre guns, all brought an unprecedented complexity to the management of naval affairs. The single-calibre, large-gunned HMS *Dreadnought*, launched in 1906, rendered all previous battleships obsolescent. And the introduction of submarines, and then aircraft, brought a third dimension to what had been hitherto a two-dimensional battle. Many new specialisations and qualifications, and some new ranks, were necessary to cope with all these innovations. Even the strategic threat turned 180 degrees about – for centuries, France had been the enemy of default and the position of the dockyards on the southern coast reflected this time-honoured reality. The formal alliance with France signed in 1904 in the face of the rising German threat necessitated the building of new dockyards and naval facilities at Rosyth, Invergordon and belatedly at Scapa Flow.

But in many ways, the Navy was an organism without a brain. There were some talented men at the top, of course, and in the early years of the new twentieth century the dynamic technocrat, Jackie Fisher, tried with limited success to make major changes. Fisher, however, believed that the essence of reform was personal dynamism untrammelled by a formal staff. Thus the Navy had to wait until 1911, after Fisher had been forced from office, before it got a naval staff. Fisher, right or wrong, was able to prevail with the 'all big gun' ship concept and the investment in torpedo-carrying craft, both surface and submarine, but his revolution remained half baked at best. Although Fisher fostered the War College set up in 1900, both as a source of friendly advice and as an educational institution, its able lecturers such as Julian Corbett found it difficult to turn the technologically minded captains into fully rounded professional practitioners of war. Mid-level officers were not encouraged to read or to educate themselves about their profession until the Royal Naval Staff College was finally formed in 1912. Thus, while there may have been a number of highly educated and able officers, the systematic study of war and teaching of its nature and its dynamics came too late to influence the Royal Navy in the First World War. Had a trained professional staff been on hand to guide it, the Admiralty might have developed a broader war-fighting doctrine, less fixated with surface action. It might also have developed equipment, training and doctrine for amphibious operations.[4] Moreover, it might not have entered the war with no minelayers, no purpose-built minesweepers, no system of night gunnery, no anti-airship gun, no anti-submarine tactics and equipment, no safe harbours, inefficient torpedoes, and only eight ships fitted with centralised director firing of the main armament.[5] But the general shortage of funds that always affect defence policy was at least some excuse for these defects, and the imperative to win the race against Germany in building capital ships was an expensive and preoccupying business with tunnel vision as one of its unfortunate results.

The arms race with Germany had impressed upon everybody the likely imminence of war, and that arms race had been won by Britain. In spite of the outpouring of men and treasure into the High Seas Fleet by Germany, Britain still had nearly two new battleships for every one of Germany's. By 1916, thirty-five dreadnoughts, the oldest of which was still only ten years old, were supported by a myriad of cruisers, destroyers and smaller craft, not to mention the numerous pre-dreadnought battleships which, although no longer able to take their place in the front line, were still useful in other less demanding roles such as shore bombardment. Ironically, they were to see more war action than their more capable successors. Thus, in spite of the lack of a formal staff to analyse requirements and produce rational responses, the Royal Navy had been receptive enough to these new developments to keep up with, and adapt to, most of the technological advances that arrived in the early twentieth century.

So the Royal Navy's early espousal of the air weapon is in itself not surprising. It was entirely consistent with the way it had adapted itself to every other technical development that the Industrial Revolution had presented to it. Flight was simply yet another technical development to be coped with, along with all the other technical developments that had been coped with hitherto. However, in order to divine why the Royal Naval Air Service was so far in advance of any other naval air service, both in quantity and quality, and arguably more technically developed than the Royal Flying Corps, it is necessary to look at wider strategic considerations, and the influence of technological advances being made many miles from the sea – on the shores of Lake Constance on the southern borders of Germany.

There was never much prospect that Germany would out-dreadnought Britain in the battleship arms race. Grand Admiral Alfred von Tirpitz, the political head of the German Navy and 'the evil genius of German foreign relations',[6] in building his fleet 'as a political power factor ... constructed so that it can unfold its greatest military potential between Heligoland and the Thames',[7] undoubtedly knew that he would strike a raw British nerve. But it was much more than that. It was a strategic error of major proportions. Nothing could have been more calculated to spook the British. For continental Germany, such a powerful fleet was in many ways a strategic luxury. It took over four long years of distant blockade to deplete the German logistical hinterland to the point where it affected her ability to wage war. On the other hand, for island Britain, freedom of the seas was a vital necessity, and when this was prejudiced during the war by submarines, she was nearly brought to her knees in a few short months. So Britain knew that she simply had to spend the resources to win the battleship race – and spend she did. Germany's fleet therefore could never be powerful enough to destroy the British Navy; and yet by building it she not only helped the war to come, but she also helped to ensure that when it did come, Britain would be on the opposing side.

Consequently there was no realistic possibility that Germany could win in an all-out confrontation with the British fleet. Her only chance would be that if she were able to identify and isolate a detached element of that fleet, she might be able to deploy a local superior force to ambush and destroy it. In this way Germany just might succeed in reducing the British superiority in numbers to a level to where an all-out confrontation might not be such a one-sided proposition. It would be guerrilla warfare at sea. The greatest difficulty with this strategy was that, in laying traps and trailing baits for detached British ships, there was always the risk that the German units would themselves fall into a counter-trap laid by the British. The side with the best knowledge of the whereabouts of the other would always have a critical advantage.

Of keen interest therefore, as to all admirals over the centuries, was the whereabouts of the opposing fleet. So long as that fleet was in port, it was possible to keep tabs on it through the use of spies. Once it left harbour, the difficulties in finding it multiplied exponentially and historically it depended on the scouting ability of the fleet to a large degree. More often than not, the alertness of the man at the top of the highest mast, and the sharpness and clarity of the vision of his Mark One eyeball, was the decider over who spotted whom first.

Tethered observation balloons had been on the inventories of a number of armies since the 1860s, but not until the twentieth century did they appear at sea. Among the first was on the Russian warship *Russ*. Originally the German passenger ship *Lahn*, she had been bought by a certain Count Stroganoff, a minor Russian royal who had fallen out of favour at the Russian court for marrying a French dancer. Stroganoff converted her at his own expense in 1904 to a captive balloon carrier, complete with balloon hangar and hydrogen gas generator, and handed her over to the Russian Navy. It was intended that she should deploy with the naval squadron bound for the Far East in early 1905 but in the event she never got there. What might have happened if the Russians had had a balloon observation capability at the battle of Tsushima in May 1905 is one of the many intriguing 'what ifs' in history.[8] Men of vision foresaw that a new dimension might be added to the equation when the Wright brothers powered their aircraft successfully in 1903. But it would be some years before powered winged flight, or heavier-than-air flight, would be reliable or flexible enough to affect directly the war at sea. Lighter-than-air flight, however, was much more advanced and offered distinct advantages to whosoever was able to avail themselves of it. Airships, because they did not depend on their locomotive power to stay aloft, had range, endurance and load-carrying capacity far beyond the winged aircraft of their day. They usually carried more than one engine – typically three – so engine failure, a not unheard of occurrence then and now, did not automatically mean descent to earth. Indeed there was every chance that they might continue with the mission. Moreover, airships could go at speeds which were not greatly exceeded by aircraft until well into the First World War. Although filled with highly flammable gas and therefore potentially vulnerable, they were capable of ascending to altitudes which rendered them virtually immune from ground-based guns. The advantages they thus offered over contemporary aircraft well into the First World War were compelling.

While the battleship-building race may have been won by Britain, Germany had a very distinct edge in the field of airships. Count Ferdinand von Zeppelin's first eponymous airship, the *Luftschiff Zeppelin 1 (LZ1)*, took to the air over Lake Constance, or the Bodensee, in 1900. Zeppelin chose to base his enterprise in a floating shed on Lake Constance in order to facilitate the alignment of the dock with the wind when docking and undocking the airship. The flight lasted less than twenty minutes before it made a forced landing on the lake. Although it flew again several times that year, Zeppelin was unable to attract any commercial interest. His financial resources became exhausted and his company was liquidated in 1901. By 1906 he had mortgaged his wife's estate and raised more money. His second aircraft, the *LZ2*, was damaged on the ground in a storm after its engines had failed, but *LZ3*, which was built by cannibalising *LZ2*, was a success and flew several thousand miles in the years leading up to war. When *LZ3* demonstrated that these machines had the potential to cruise reliably over long distances, the German Army started taking an interest in them. In 1908 they bought *LZ3* and, over the next six years, more than twenty further Zeppelins were built for military and civil purposes. The Zeppelin story is punctuated with accidents and disasters but, as with fixed-wing flight, men had sufficient vision and faith to continue in the face of all the setbacks. Some machines were turned over for commercial use but by 1908, Zeppelin airships were an established feature in the German military inventory. At the outbreak of the First World War, Germany was known to have eleven Zeppelins available to her armed forces, with more under construction.

To begin with, the German Army had no clear idea of the military potential of the Zeppelin, or how they might use them to best effect. The German Navy was even less enlightened. Tirpitz did not want to divert resources from his beloved High Seas Fleet to new technologies. The German Navy did not take possession of its first Zeppelin until 1912 and it promptly crashed the following year, as did its successor. A third naval airship only entered service in 1914. No such accusation can be made of the British Navy, which recognised the possibilities of airships long before their counterparts in Germany. For them the stakes were high. Unless or until the British developed their own airship, or a means of countering the German airships, the Zeppelin seemed to offer the German Navy a reconnaissance asset of inestimable value. They were what we now call a 'force multiplier'. Here was a means of negating the British superiority in numbers of battleships at a fraction of the cost.

British officialdom was at first cautious towards the implications of the conquest of the air. However, in 1907, an airship built for the Army called *Nulli Secundus* had flown over St Paul's and Buckingham Palace, exciting public interest. From this time, an increasingly influential body of opinion was seized by the vulnerability of London to aerial attack. Meanwhile, 'the policy of the government with regard to all branches of aerial navigation was based on a desire to keep in touch with the movement rather than to hasten its development. It was felt that we stood to gain nothing by forcing a means of warfare which tended to reduce the value of our insular position and the protection of our sea power.'[9]

Nevertheless, as soon as flight had been seriously demonstrated in Europe in 1908, the Committee of Imperial Defence called for a study led by Lord Esher into 'the dangers to which we would be exposed on sea or on land by any developments in aerial navigation reasonably probable in the near future'.[10] This committee, which reported in January 1909, correctly identified all the risks that Britain might face in future from enemy aircraft: the insertion of airborne raiding forces, and the bombing of warships, dockyards, arsenals and other vital facilities. It also pointed out that: 'It seems certain that even in their existing state of development, dirigible balloons might be employed in naval warfare to ascertain the movements of fleets and to give warning of attack. No means can at present be suggested for preventing this.' The committee then went on to recommend that 'the evidence before the Committee tends to show that the full potentialities of the airships, and the dangers to which we might be exposed by their use, can only be ascertained by building them ourselves.'[11]

Also in 1908, the public mood was stimulated by H.G. Wells who published a serialised science fiction thriller, *The War in the Air*, which envisaged a devastating attack by German airships on New York. In the book, this assault draws all the world's major powers into a series of aerial wars with each other, bringing widespread destruction and constant guerrilla warfare as the breakdown of civilisation and a new dark age descends on the planet. The book was couched in language calculated to wind up anxiety over the potential destructive power and menace that aircraft and airships might bring. Fanciful and jejune even for its own time, nevertheless like much science fiction, Wells's book was in many ways merely ahead of its time. The devastation and destruction that he describes in his air raids was recognisably similar to that produced by the Allied bombing raids on Germany and Japan in the Second World War. In 1908, with the German Army buying its first airship, many people feared that Wells's vision of total war could come true in the uncomfortably close future. Furthermore, he describes how the airships observe, with an all-seeing eye, a naval battle in the North Atlantic, and how they intervene and damage an American battleship. For the British, who had laid out vast treasures on their battle fleets, and placed great store by them, this albeit fictional suggestion of vulnerability of the battleship gave them much to think about.

Less widely read but of greater long-term influence were the ideas of the Italian Colonel Giuilo Douhet which were published the following year. Douhet foretold in more measured terms how airpower would transform the conduct of war. No longer would there be clearly defined fronts and battle lines. Aircraft would reach with impunity behind the lines and bring about the end of wars by destroying the soldiers' means to fight.

In 1909 the Aerial League of the British Empire was founded, which further goaded the government for its apparent lack of air policy. Louis Blériot's cross-Channel flight in July 1909 did nothing to reduce the pressure. It took him twenty-five minutes to cross the ditch that had insulated Britain from the Continent for millennia and there was nothing anyone could have done to stop him. For many, Blériot's risky adventure in a tiny fragile machine was a disquieting omen. The moat had been breached. It was reported that the Germans were exploring the possibility of using airships in an offensive role and, moreover, that a German artillery expert, General Rohme,[12] felt that the best counter to airships were other airships. Everything seemed to be going the airship's way.

The aeroplane, however, could not be ignored. After Orville and Wilbur Wright achieved the first man-controlled heavier-than-air powered flight in December 1903 among the sand dunes of North Carolina, they went back home to Dayton and continued to develop their machine in secrecy while they sought patents for their pioneering work. The effect of this secrecy was more negative than positive as it obscured the level of their success. By the following year they had achieved flights of 24 miles distance lasting over half an hour and still the world did not know. When the time came to offer the patents for sale, no one was interested: not the US government, not the French government, and certainly not the British government which was offered the patent three times between 1906 and 1908. In 1908, Wilbur Wright brought one of their latest machines to France and put on a performance that flabbergasted the natives. Eventually a French syndicate bought the patents. But before the syndicate could reap the reward of its investment, two French pioneers, Henry Farman and Léon Delagrange, disregarding niceties such as patents, had built their own machines. In spite of a series of lawsuits, the genie was now out of the bottle. 'From this time onwards, the progress of flying was rapid and immense. A great industry came into being, and, after a short time, ceased to pay any tribute whatever to the inventors.'[13]

As the Admiralty considered its response to the epochal events of 1908 it was clear that the large rigid airship was the only option for an aerial platform that could operate for extended periods with, and in support of, the fleet at sea. Today an expensive study would have delayed matters; then the response was quicker. In 1909, the Admiralty awarded a contract to Messrs Vickers, Son & Maxim at Barrow-in-Furness to build for them a dirigible airship. Vickers had had no experience with airships but they had been successful builders of early submarines – also long tubular structures capable of three-dimensional movement in a fluid medium – and perhaps it was assumed that this would stand them in good stead when it came to building airships. Indeed, in some aspects, the project was very advanced. The frames and cross members were made of an aluminium and copper alloy called duralumin. Not until 1914 did the Zeppelin manufacturers take advantage of the strength and lightness this material offered. The now familiar mooring mast was also a concept pioneered by Vickers. This airship was widely, if unofficially, known as the *Mayfly*, which suggests that there may have been doubt about the viability of the project from the start. The mayfly is in fact an insect of the Order Ephemeroptera, which in Greek means 'short lived'. Mayflies live for a few hours or, at most, a few days. In the event the name was strangely appropriate. The *Mayfly* never flew. She proved too heavy and had to be lightened by weakening her structure. Then her back was broken irreparably by a gust of wind while reversing her out of her shed in September 1911.

The situation was ironical. The Royal Navy wanted airships but British industry could not build them. German industry could build more or less successful airships but the Imperial German Navy did not want them – yet. Britain went back to the drawing board and was not to have successful rigid airships until she copied shot-down Zeppelins during the war.

An alternative path was opening up, however. Following this airship failure, three naval officers, Lieutenants Samson, Gregory and Longmore, and one Royal Marine Light Infantry officer, Lieutenant Gerrard, were sent to the civilian flying school at Eastchurch on the Island of Sheppey to learn how to fly. And so Royal Naval heavier-than-air aviation was born.

The Royal Navy of those days sometimes appears to us to have been a deeply conservative club: a warm, rich, breeding soil for stuffy martinets, and that it surely was, but there were corners which were sufficiently fresh and vital to attract and give oxygen to some remarkably able, energetic and far-sighted men. Fisher himself, although something of an unguided missile, was a powerful agent for change. There were many others across the Service who, seeing the risks and possibilities in aviation, realised that the Royal Navy simply must get to grips with it. No one was more seized with its importance than Captain Murray Sueter. Sueter was an imaginative, dynamic innovator with a strong technical bent. He had worked extensively with early torpedoes and submarines and had been placed in charge of the team which had been set up to assist Vickers in the construction of the *Mayfly*. After the failure of that project, he had returned to general service with his men.

Later that year, 1911, in the face of the heavier-than-air developments in France and the lighter-than-air developments in Germany, the government charged another committee with advising it on the development of British military aviation generally. Sueter was called to give evidence. In his statement he foresaw the development of seaplanes as well as naval airships. He was emphatic that the 'problem of the air was vital to the Navy ... we must command the air. I do not say that we wish to do so, but I think we will be forced to do so.' Captain Bertram Dickson also submitted written evidence: 'The efforts which each side would exert in order to hinder or prevent the enemy from obtaining information... would lead to the inevitable result of a war in the air, for the supremacy of the air, by armed aeroplanes against each other. This fight for the supremacy of the air in future wars will be of the first and greatest importance.'

The Army meanwhile had formed, first a Balloon School, and then an Air Battalion of Royal Engineers. The result of the committee's deliberations was that the resources of both Services would be formalised and drawn together under one umbrella, and on 8 April 1912, the Royal Flying Corps was formed. The paper which was the basis for this decision was written by army officers and in practice, the new corps was distinctly orientated towards the Army. The new corps had a Central Flying School at Upavon and two wings: a Military Wing and a Naval Wing. An Aircraft Factory was also established at Farnborough with the intention of supplying machines for both wings. It was intended that this new force should be a stand-alone separate Service in much the same way as the

Royal Air Force eventually became. 'The British Aeronautical Service should be regarded as one and should be designated "The Flying Corps".'[14] An 'air committee' was established to deal with all aeronautical questions affecting both the Admiralty and the War Office, but it was essentially a consultative body with no executive powers. It was certainly not in a position to adjudicate between the Army and the Navy. Neither could it counter the centrifugal forces that were bound to develop.

The original idea was that in a naval war, the aircraft and men of the Military Wing would operate in support of the Naval Wing, and vice versa in the case of a land war.[15] This elegant and apparently worthy expression of mutual support helps to explain why the two wings never sat comfortably beside each other. The idea that an aircraft flown by a pilot trained to support land forces with reconnaissance could, on demand, switch to support naval forces, demonstrates that the authors of this policy had no idea of the manifold complexities and hazards of maritime aviation.

The range, reliability and load-carrying capability of these primitive machines allowed only tactical reconnaissance on land to be contemplated in the immediate future. Perhaps this fact set the Royal Flying Corps off along a predominantly military path, a path it was not seriously to be deviated from until the two Services were to unite again on 1 April 1918 with the formation of the Royal Air Force. Naval aviation on the other hand presented a whole new set of threats and technical challenges which tended to take second place until the difficulties of flying over land had been mastered. Here the sea was the greatest enemy. Numerous early aviators simply disappeared without trace at sea and there were many factors which might conspire to make that happen. Navigation was then far more difficult on its featureless seascape. The weather tends to be more violent and changeable at sea, and a forced landing put the aviator in a very different set of circumstances than those he might find himself in were he able to come down in a convenient field. And even if one was equipped to land at sea, restarting an engine on anything but the flattest of calms was highly problematical. Moreover, supposing one had landed in one piece, but could not take off, one's chances of survival still depended on the timely arrival of a rescuing surface vessel. Early maritime aviators carried pigeons in the hope that they would be able to initiate a rescue with their message. In addition, ships move far more quickly than land formations, and information gathered at sea needed to be imparted in a timely fashion if it was to be of any use, so it is no surprise that it was the Navy that first pioneered the fitting of radios in their aircraft. Work with radios progressed to the point whereby naval aircraft were routinely carrying radios by the outbreak of war.

Thus, the concept that army aviators could switch at will to operating in the maritime environment would never have occurred to a sailor.

The first army commanders of the Royal Flying Corps could not be expected to be familiar with the maritime environment which was so different to their own experience. Furthermore, one should never underestimate the influence of personalities and relationships, and their importance at this early juncture was momentous. Brigadier General David Henderson was the Royal Flying Corps' first commander and he had played a crucial part in the process leading up to its formation. He was an army officer with strong views about the purposes of military aviation. He had been the Director of Military Intelligence in the Boer War in South Africa and had become one of the leading authorities in tactical intelligence. His experience in this field doubtless informed his belief that the central function of the aeroplane was to support land forces, chiefly by conducting aerial reconnaissance. The commander of the Military Wing from the outbreak of war was Hugh Trenchard. (Did any man's name ever better evoke his personality than Trenchard's?) He was to become known as 'the father of the Royal Air Force' – a title more properly accorded to Henderson – and by extension, every other air force besides, but at this stage in his career, Trenchard was also vigorously of the view that aircraft were best used in support of land forces. His vision was broader than Henderson's in that he believed in the offensive role of air power, but this did not extend to the strategic offensive. His predecessor was another army officer, Frederick Sykes. Sykes was probably the most versatile and far sighted of the senior men in the Royal Flying Corps. A cavalry officer, he was nevertheless to be sent to Gallipoli in 1915 to rationalise the Royal Naval Air Service in that theatre. His report was found to be most valuable, and he was made a temporary colonel of Royal Marines and placed in command with conspicuous success for the remainder of the campaign. Meanwhile, in 1914, he was Henderson's chief of staff when the Royal Flying Corps went to France. The chemistry between him, Trenchard and Henderson seems to have been toxic. Sykes's vision was wider than both Henderson's and Trenchard's and he was a proponent of bombing, but Trenchard, the older of the two, hated and despised Sykes in spite of his 'high intelligence and great charm'.[16] Trenchard did everything he could to marginalise Sykes for the rest of his career.

Henderson too distrusted Sykes, believing that Sykes had ambitions to displace him. It was the imprint of Henderson and Trenchard that the Royal Flying Corps bore most clearly from its earliest days. That personalities like these did not always see eye to eye with men like Churchill and Sueter comes as no surprise. What is more surprising is that Henderson's views prevailed in spite of the need to counter the Zeppelin and protect Great Britain, the original threat which had spurred the government into forming the Royal Flying Corps in the first place. The progress from articulation of government policy to practical military implementation of that policy seems to have taken an astonishingly disjointed turn and the Military Wing of the Royal Flying Corps ignored the Zeppelin completely.

These considerations, together with the Royal Engineer pedigree of the new formation, tended to separate rather than unite the two wings. The failure to appoint an 'air board', chaired by a government minister answerable for the new Service to the Cabinet, in the same way that the two existing Services were governed, allowed this tendency of drifting apart to continue unchecked. Such a body could have formulated and directed a coherent over-arching air policy, as indeed it did later when the Royal Air Force was eventually formed in 1918. But in 1912 the Air Committee had no such powers and an air board didn't exist, so the two Services were left to pursue their own divergent interests.

From the beginning, the Royal Flying Corps focussed its efforts on co-operating with and supporting the Army with reconnaissance. It was believed that the best aircraft for this purpose should be slow and stable. Henderson's fixation with reconnaissance led him to place a limit of 100 horsepower on the aero engines produced for the Military Wing, and so the Royal Flying Corps entered the war with a portfolio of slow, stable aircraft entirely unsuited for anything other than unopposed reconnaissance. The Navy's direct interest in countering the Zeppelin, on the other hand, helped to induce a wider view of aviation. This included an understanding of the possibilities for offensive action, and they set about developing an appropriate capability.

With the Army's needs so predominant, the Naval Wing started to cut its own furrow right from the inception of the Royal Flying Corps. They bypassed the Central Flying School which was intended for both Services, continued to train their own pilots at Eastchurch and, instead of placing orders with the Aircraft Factory, they dealt with private commercial companies as they did with their other technical equipment. By 1913, the Naval Wing of the Royal Flying Corps had become generally known as the Royal Naval Air Service and was doing its own thing with little or no reference either to the Military Wing or the mainstream Admiralty. It occupied its own privileged bureaucratic space protected by the First Lord, Winston Churchill.

In the two years remaining before the outbreak of war things moved fast for aviation in the Royal Navy. Shortly after the formation of the Royal Flying Corps in April 1912, Captain Murray Sueter and the supervisor of the Aircraft Factory, Mr Mervyn O'Gorman, visited several countries in Europe including Germany. This visit, which included a flight in the latest Zeppelin, the *Viktoria Luise*, made a deep impression on them. First hand, they discovered the advanced nature of German aviation and, in particular, they gained a clear and vivid picture of the threat that the Zeppelin presented.

Everything about the Zeppelin was impressive. The *Viktoria Luise* was in commercial use but, at the time of Sueter's and O'Gorman's flight, the first ill-fated, exclusively naval machine was being built to similar specifications. The airship was over 500 feet long and was sustained in the air by nearly 800,000 cubic feet of hydrogen in eighteen gas cells or bags which were contained within an envelope covering a rigid frame of girders and cross members. The lift available for fuel, crew and warlike stores was over 20,000lb. It had three engines and four propellers – one of the engines powered two propellers – which drove it at 47 mph. It protected itself with several machine guns, some of which could be mounted on the top of the envelope. A typical bomb load was between 3,000 and 5,000lb. By October 1914, the Germans already had bombs weighing 110lb in service and in December that year they dropped their first experimental whopper of 660lb. The heaviest bomb in the British inventory at that time was nominally 20lb. It in fact weighed slightly less than that. On the other hand a heavier bomb would have been little use to the British as they had nothing that could have lifted it. By the end of the war, both the British and the German navies had large seaplanes with twelve hours endurance in the air. But in 1914, a Zeppelin could travel over a 1,000 miles and stay aloft for over a day and a half. These figures were handsomely exceeded in due course by later marks which had six or seven engines, were to achieve speeds of nearly 80 mph and were to have bomb loads of over 9,000lb. From mid-1916, Zeppelins were being built that could carry nearly 5 tons of bombs and had ten machine guns with which to defend themselves. Not until well into the Second World War were fixed-wing aircraft able to carry such bomb loads. Even today, the Panavia Tornado typically carries a bomb load similar to that of the 1916 Zeppelin.

The gas bags were made from the membrane taken from the intestines of cattle and were very gas-tight. It took around 50,000 cattle to make one gas cell and so they were very expensive. These membranes were imported from Argentina, a factor which came to be a serious problem once the British naval blockade made an impact later in the war. Hydrogen is the lightest known gas and easily manufactured, but it is highly flammable, and, when mixed with air, it is explosive. Great care was taken to ensure hydrogen gas purity, and between flights the gas cells were kept full and under positive pressure to avoid contamination with air. Helium, which has 93 per cent of hydrogen's lifting power, is inert. But helium is a product of natural gas, to which the Germans had no access during the war.

Being supported by a highly flammable gas was the dirigible's Achilles heel. But they were still difficult to shoot down. Ordinary bullets made holes but did not set them alight, and it took a lot of holes to affect the performance of a compartmentalised envelope of nearly half a million cubic feet. So difficult to destroy were they that the British thought erroneously that they must have a protective outer envelope of inert exhaust gas from the engines. Only when tracer and other incendiary weapons were developed did they regularly fall in flames. The Zeppelin's chief protection was its ability to climb more quickly and to greater altitudes than aeroplanes. As aircraft capabilities improved as the war progressed, so did the Zeppelin's ability to climb. The later Zeppelins could climb at a rate of 1,000 feet per minute and ascend routinely to heights of over 20,000 feet. Few aircraft were able to match this. The best chance for an aircraft against a Zeppelin was to surprise it at the lower altitudes at which it had to fly to be remotely effective.

To begin with, all dirigibles were built by Zeppelin's company based at Friedrichshafen on Lake Constance. From early 1915, a second company, the Luftschiffbau Schütte-Lanz GmbH of Mannheim-Rheinau, also manufactured them. The principal difference was that the latter used aspen-based plywood instead of duralumin in the construction of the frames. Zeppelin was the preferred manufacturer for both the Army and the Navy, neither having any great enthusiasm for the Schütte-Lanz products, although the Army probably disliked them less overtly than the Navy. Both were known generically as Zeppelins in Britain and elsewhere.

The infrastructure necessary to support these machines was no less impressive than the crafts themselves. The airships required hangars which were not unlike Victorian railway stations in scale. The later ones were 110 feet high, 200 feet wide and 800 feet long, and a small number were built on a revolving axis in order to adjust to the wind while moving the Zeppelins in and out. The manpower requirement was also prodigious. Each airship had a crew of around twenty men and, because they stayed in the air for prolonged periods, they operated in watches or shifts. However, to walk an airship in and out of its hangar required a ground crew of 300 or 400 men. A total of fifteen airship bases was used, although the principal seven were concentrated in the littoral close to the north German coast. The Zeppelins were a huge investment, but once the infrastructure was in place, it was possible to build a Zeppelin in six weeks. A cruiser took two years. At the time of Sueter's flight, much of this was in the future. But Sueter could see the potential. He also knew that, somewhat belatedly, the German Navy had started turning that potential into reality, and that, until Britain developed an effective counter, the German Navy had a critical scouting and reconnaissance edge over the Royal Navy at sea. The Germans had potential air supremacy.

Sueter and O'Gorman reported to the same committee that gave birth to the Royal Flying Corps. The committee concluded that:

> In any future war with Germany, except in foggy or stormy weather, it is probable that no British war vessels or torpedo craft will be able to approach within many miles of the German coast without their presence being discovered ... In favourable weather, German airships can already be employed for reconnaissance over vast areas of the North Sea, and one airship, owing to the extended view from high altitudes, under favourable weather conditions, is able to accomplish the work of a large number of scouting cruisers. It is difficult to exaggerate the value of this advantage to Germany.[17]

It was also pointed out that Zeppelins could carry a bomb load which might threaten ships, docks, power stations and other infrastructure, and that they were far less dependent on favourable weather than was generally supposed. In comparison, Britain's air force comprised a small number of very basic aeroplanes and two small airships.

It would not have been surprising if the admirals and politicians who read this report had felt a cold chill run down their spines. They had committed by far the greater part of Britain's defence resources towards building a navy of battleships which stayed comfortably ahead of every other navy, in particular the Imperial German Navy, and now it looked as if the German Navy had bested them at a fraction of the cost. As early as 1909, there was a fear that a fleet of Zeppelins might suddenly appear and launch a devastating raid against the Royal Navy at anchor; Zeppelins to which they had no effective counter and which they could not begin to match. Neither would they have derived any comfort from the report of General Jimmy Grierson who noted after an exercise using balloons and aircraft equipped with primitive radios to spy on the enemy:

> their use has revolutionised the art of war. So long as hostile aircraft are hovering over one's troops, all movements are liable to be seen and reported, and therefore the first step in war will be to get rid of the hostile aircraft. He who does this first, or who keeps the last aeroplane afloat, will win, other things being approximately equal.

If the Royal Navy wanted long-range aircraft it had no alternative but to persevere with whatever airships it could lay its hands upon. The only airships Britain could build were non-rigids – effectively large balloons – and thus less capable than the larger multiple-gas-cell rigids. The factory which had built the Army non-rigids was commissioned to build a similar one for the Navy, and the Army's existing airships were handed over to the Royal Naval Air Service. But the expertise for building the airships they really needed was abroad, chiefly in Germany. The Germans were not about to manufacture Zeppelins for the British, so Vickers were again contracted to build two rigid airships for the Navy. Six smaller non-rigid airships were also commissioned, four from British manufacturers, one from Italy and one from Germany. None of these were complete by the outbreak of war and unsurprisingly, the Germans confiscated the one under construction in Germany. The Italians did the same. The non-rigid airships under construction in Britain were eventually completed but the rigid programme was suspended for a time. So once more, by the outbreak of war, the British attempt to match the Germans capability like for like was thwarted.

But matters had not been standing still on the naval heavier-than-air front. Even in the earliest years of aviation, there were those who could see that heavier-than-air flight offered infinitely greater potential in the long run. The most senior of these was Winston Churchill. Churchill, who had become First Lord of the Admiralty in October 1911, was a gifted, imaginative dynamo; he was also a meddler and a gambler. For every shaft of brilliance he produced, there was another less-than-fully-baked idea. What the Navy really needed was a clear-sighted professional organiser to transform it into a modern war-fighting machine. What it got was an energetic, flamboyant amateur who was somewhat seduced by the glory of being the titular head of the biggest navy in the world. However, it is doubtful if any one man could have shaken the Navy into shape in peacetime – it took the lethal stimulus of war to do that. But in areas where Churchill's enthusiasm was gripped, his intervention could be especially fruitful. Naval aviation was one such happy instance.

Churchill was persuaded to take a flight in an aeroplane in 1912 and was entranced. He loved it, was invigorated by the dangers, and stimulated and fascinated by the possibilities. He received flying instructions and was on the point of taking his flying certificate when, under pressure from his friends and in the face of pleadings from his pregnant wife, he desisted. He never qualified as a pilot but he was thereafter unambiguous and articulate in his belief in the superiority and long-term potential of the aeroplane. Churchill was never one to be satisfied with his own job alone. He always took an active interest in matters of detail well below his pay grade, which although probably irritating and disturbing for his admirals, almost certainly gave life and vigour to matters which otherwise might have moved at only the most pedestrian pace. He also attempted to look forward. He wasn't always right, but in the case of the Royal Naval Air Service, he was spot on. He foresaw pressing operational and strategic requirements far beyond the mere tactical reconnaissance roles upon which the Royal Flying Corps had largely set its sights. He recommended new types of aircraft to meet these requirements, calling for aircraft designed for scouting and fighting over the sea, and for aircraft to operate from aircraft carriers. He became the Royal Naval Air Service's most powerful and passionate sponsor and advocate.

Churchill had his own ideas about how to deal with the Zeppelin threat. In a paper written in October 1913, he described how fighters were required to defend Britain against air attack on vulnerable points. He postulated how an aeroplane should attack the Zeppelin by descending obliquely from above and discharging a series of small bombs or fireballs at rapid intervals. This called for aircraft with an excellent rate of climb and the ability to drop bombs. Strictly speaking he was correct, but at the time he said it, there was no aircraft which was up to the task, and as he later acknowledged, 'we were not in a position at the beginning of the war to produce effective results.'[18]

At the outbreak of war it was still held by many that airships were the pre-eminent means of aerial warfare. With a working payload of over 10 tons, they were capable of carrying radios, bombs, cameras, observers and machine guns, and they had vastly superior range and endurance. By ditching ballast, they had the ability to ascend at high speed to altitudes greater than that of the aeroplane. And they suffered no great disadvantage in speed. Zeppelins were also to prove remarkably difficult to destroy from the air. Not until June 1915 was the first airborne Zeppelin destroyed by an aircraft. It demanded great courage and resourcefulness, and the pilot, Flight Sub Lieutenant Reginald Warneford of the Royal Naval Air Service, had to push his aircraft and its engine to the very limits of what it could take. He had tried to attack it with his carbine but had been driven off by defensive machine-gun fire. He eventually managed to get above the Zeppelin, which was at 6,000 feet, and dived steeply to within 60 feet of the top of it while under fire from the machine gunner stationed on the upper surface of the dirigible. He dropped three bombs which had the desired effect. In the subsequent explosion, Warneford was singed and stunned, while his aircraft was damaged and tossed out of control. Recovering while his aircraft was in a precipitous dive, he managed to land in a field in German-held territory. With one of his petrol tanks holed and a fuel line severed, he made some running repairs, which included using his cigarette holder to connect the broken ends of his fuel pipe. He swung his own propeller and dived into the cockpit as the plane trundled off downhill, with Germans firing at him. He then got lost in the mist and landed on the foreshore at Cap Griz Nez where he was taken prisoner by French soldiers until they were finally convinced that he was on their side.[19]

Warneford was awarded the Victoria Cross and there was much jubilation at this success, his face appearing in cinema screens throughout the Empire, the jubliation being directly proportional to the fear and foreboding that the Zeppelins had hitherto induced.

Warneford's feat was achieved over Belgium. It was not until September 1916, two years into the war, that the first Zeppelin to be destroyed over British soil was shot down in an air-to-air encounter. Air defence of the United Kingdom had by now been taken over by the Army and the Royal Flying Corps. The pilot, Lieutenant Leefe-Robinson, was on a night sortie over London and had attempted to shoot one Zeppelin down at long range, but it escaped into heavy fog. There were thirteen airships over London that night and when he found a second one at 11,000 feet, he poured automatic fire into it and it soon began to burn. After a little while, it started to fall to earth in flames. It took over two minutes to descend nearly 2 miles, a spectacular, hellish, incandescent pyre, watched with fascinated, horrified delight by many citizens of London. Lieutenant William Leefe-Robinson also won a Victoria Cross.

But at the beginning of the war, the question of how to defeat and destroy Zeppelins was an issue of great concern. Pilots themselves acknowledged the difficulties they faced, and some were ready to take extreme measures because they thought they might be necessary. 'Any pilot who met a Zeppelin and failed to bring it down by firing at it, would be expected to take other measures, that is to say, to charge it. Not a few of the early war pilots were prepared to carry out these instructions.'[20]

Furthermore the British public was seized with an apprehension about Zeppelins which was far removed from reality. The press, then as now, recognising that there is nothing quite like a good bout of public hysteria for selling newspapers, did nothing to reduce the tension. Fanciful reports of Zeppelin sightings abounded. Like modern reports of 'flying saucers' and other unidentified flying objects, newspapers and magazines milked these for what they were worth. Consequently these large, menacing, sinister monsters loomed ever larger and ever more threatening in the public's perception.[21] Germany's success, and Britain's failure to build them, lent weight to the belief of German superior technology. It was assumed that H.G. Wells's novel *The War in the Air* would become a reality, and fleets of Zeppelins would rain devastation on Britain as soon as the Kaiser found it convenient to give the order. The nerve centres of government and defence would be eliminated: parliament and other vital centres; oil refineries and storage depots, lock gates, dockyards, railway stations; ammunition dumps, and so on. All were exposed to sudden and complete destruction. It was rumoured that the Germans estimated that it was possible to fly 350,000 men in Zeppelins across the Channel in one night.

Reality took a back seat in these considerations, with the difficulties that Zeppelins faced rarely being taken into account. Bad weather, bombing inaccuracy, navigation difficulties, mechanical failure and the fact that Germany only possessed very few machines – these and other limitations were never allowed to constrain the outpourings of doom and gloom.

It is difficult for us today to understand why people felt so strongly, and had such truly fantastic – even absurd – ideas so distant from reality. The British, whose paranoia was unrestrained by any experience of the technical and practical limitations of Zeppelin airships, could only see the horrors that they portended. Aerial navigation, perhaps because it had intrigued men's imagination for so long, tended to trigger an excitement, even a hysteria, wholly out of proportion with reality. Public passions in Britain based on ignorance and fed by the media arose, comparable to that engendered by the infernal weaving machines of the eighteenth century or by genetically modified foods, or terrorism today.

The British were not the only ones who were deluded. The German Deputy Chief of Naval Staff was also of the opinion that attacks on London and the main naval bases would cause a panic so great that the British would have to abandon the war. No doubt the excessive British pessimism helped to feed a reciprocal German optimism. There also existed the outlandish notion that explosives dropped from the air would somehow behave differently than when fired from a gun. It was felt in some quarters that the destructive effect of air-delivered normal explosives would be a thousand times greater. It was as if by dropping explosives from aircraft, they would somehow behave like nuclear weapons. British hysteria was matched in Germany by wholly unrealistic ideas of what might be achieved by aerial bombing. For one thing, instead of having fleets of the monsters, there was only a small number operational at the beginning of the war, although others were on the stocks. In fact, in the German Navy, those who had a first-hand understanding of the dangers and the practical, technical limitations associated with managing and running them, were less than enthusiastic about them. The disasters that overtook the first naval Zeppelins had a serious impact. The third naval Zeppelin had entered service in May 1914, but the first two had been lost the previous autumn. The first one crashed in the sea in a storm; only six of the crew of twenty survived. The second, a brand-new machine, suffered a catastrophic fire in the air before she was even commissioned into service and crashed killing all twenty-eight on board. Those forty-eight men represented the core of the German Navy's expertise and their loss was a severe blow. Although five more naval Zeppelins were brought into service before 1914 was out, and others existed in the Army and in commercial service, the German Navy had only one operational dirigible in August 1914.

Captain Sueter, notwithstanding his involvement with the *Mayfly* project and his first-hand knowledge of the German Zeppelin capability, was another of those far and clear-sighted men who advocated heavier-than-air aviation. He saw the value of airships, notably in the anti-submarine role, but was especially forceful in his work in support of aircraft and their utility in the maritime environment. By 1912, Sueter was Director of the Air Department of the Admiralty. Under Churchill's enthusiastic, flamboyant, political patronage, Sueter set about making up lost ground. The first four naval pilots had been trained to fly at Eastchurch on the Isle of Sheppey in a civilian establishment owned by a Mr Frank McClean the year before. Frank McClean, through his ownership of Eastchurch and his open-handed support and instruction of naval pilots, was to become an important figure in early British naval aviation.

One of these first pilots whom he trained was Lieutenant Charles Samson. Second perhaps only to Sueter, Samson was to do more than any other officer to further the development of early naval flying. He was a courageous, dynamic, restless officer and a powerful, charismatic leader. On completion of his pilot's course in 1911, he persuaded the Admiralty to buy Mr McLean's aeroplanes and to establish a naval flying school at Eastchurch. His persuasive talents were no doubt assisted by the fact that he was a friend of Winston Churchill. He it was who had persuaded Churchill to take his first flight in 1912, and in doing so he lit a flame that was to burn brightly and with great consequence for the next half century. A full-scale training programme was set in place and the call for trainee pilots went out to the Fleet. There was no shortage of fine volunteers, but as so often happens, commanding officers were sometimes reluctant to let their best men go and only supplied those whom they were happy to get rid of. 'If they don't break their necks, it will wake them up.'[22] But overall, the quality of the material supplied was very high.

Samson then embarked on a series of experiments in Chatham dockyard. He put a trackway on top of the 12-inch guns in the forward gun turret of the battleship HMS *Africa* and launched himself into the air successfully in December 1911. Then, with the help of the aircraft manufacturer Horace Short, he designed a seaplane which he flew successfully at Portland in March 1912. He wasn't the first to take off from the water but, with this particular aircraft, he started a partnership between Shorts and the Navy that was to produce a rich portfolio of aircraft in both World Wars and beyond. In due course Samson pioneered flying at night with no lights on either the aircraft or the airfield, and much else besides. Practical experiment, trial and error, more experiment, and then some success characterised the life of the pilots and supporting crews.

They kept in touch with their brother aviators in the Military Wing of the Royal Flying Corps who were also pushing out the boundaries of their knowledge and experience daily. Some of their discoveries to us today may appear charming, or even hilarious. For instance, it was important to know which way the wind was blowing on the ground before one came in to land. If there were trees or bushes about, then well and good. But in the absence of these, animal indicators could be used. It was observed that cows, when grazing in a field, presumably in order to avoid experiencing the benefits of their own famous flatulence, all seemed to face into wind. However daft this may sound to us, it seems they were on to something. Grazing animals are now known to face in a way which optimises the benefit they get from the sun or the wind, depending on the prevailing environment. However, a recent study indicates that cows may also be magnetosensitive,[23] which means that they tend to point north-south, or south-north. So it seems that there were other factors abroad which might have complicated the calculations of earlier aviators of which they were unaware. The sheep altimeter test was also deemed useful. Landing was usually the moment fraught with most danger and it was important to be able to judge one's height in the final moments. Altimeters were crude and unreliable at low heights, but if there were sheep around, they could help. Above a certain height, sheep ignored the early aeroplanes. Below a certain height, they bolted. It was reckoned that the moment when they turned to look just before they bolted was about 350 feet. Whether farting cows were useful wind-direction indicators, or bolting sheep were more dependable than altimeters, must remain open to question.

The approach to learning to fly was rather like learning to drive, or learning a language. One took as many lessons as was thought necessary and then took the test. This could take a few weeks, or in the case of a driven man in a hurry, a great deal less. A certain passed-over major of the Royal Scots Fusiliers, one Hugh Trenchard, having turned to flying to escape from a dead-end infantry career at the age of thirty-nine, was under pressure to get his wings before he passed over the age limit at forty. He did it in a week; six weeks later he was a flying instructor. Noel Pemberton Billing, of whom more later, succeeded in learning to fly and qualifying for his flying certificate in less than twenty-four hours for a £500 bet. In fact, he was only in the air for a little over four hours. But even he was a slow learner compared to Bugler Arthur Harris of the 1st Rhodesian Regiment. Harris, who was to become the most famous 'bomber' of them all, had returned to the United Kingdom to enlist in the British forces upon the disbandment of his regiment in Rhodesia. He failed to find a place in the cavalry or the artillery and so in 1915 applied for the Royal Flying Corps. Meanwhile, he set about learning to fly on his own account. The tuition time deemed sufficient for him to qualify as civilian pilot was half an hour.[24]

They had no parachutes. This applied to all fliers of all the belligerents on both sides for the first three years of war. One feels compelled to ask why this should have been so as parachutes had been in existence since the 1880s. They had been successfully trialled from aircraft in 1912 and they were issued right from the beginning of the war to men in the tethered observation balloons that were used to direct artillery near the front line. These were of the 'attached' type, namely they were fixed to the balloon basket with a static line. When the balloonist jumped, his weight hauled the 'chute from its container, and it deployed. If the balloonist left it too late, there was the risk that the balloon basket would fall at the same time as the balloonist, in which case his parachute could not deploy; or that his flaming balloon would fall on him and bring him and his parachute catastrophically down to earth. But balloons were easy sitting targets for aircraft and about 800 balloonists' lives were saved by their parachutes.

Technical difficulties have been cited as the reason why parachutes were not issued to pilots. The early versions of the inventor Everard Calthrop's 'Guardian Angel' weighed 90lb. In an Avro 504 of 1914, this weight amounted to more than the entire bomb load of the aircraft. Although Calthrop's next version weighed only 24lb and required a mere 100 feet to deploy, this parachute was relatively bulky and had to be stowed outside the cockpit. It thereby affected the aerodynamics and had a consequent adverse influence on the performance of early aircraft. Nevertheless, as aircraft and engines became more and more capable as the war progressed, there was a stunning absence of progress towards what seems to us a compelling necessity.

It is clear that if the authorities on both sides had wanted to provide their pilots with effective parachutes during the First World War, it could have been done without sacrificing undue performance or payload, and at a relatively minor cost. A number of pilots tried to supply themselves with parachutes but were prevented from doing so. An experienced and highly decorated man like Major Mick Mannock claimed that, because he was unable to carry a parachute, he carried a revolver to finish himself off as soon as he saw the first signs of flames. In 1918, the Germans did finally start to use parachutes and yet still British officialdom remained unmoved. Committees were formed to study the question, and trials were conducted, but the result was the same. Why, when men at sea were routinely supplied with life jackets, were men in the air not given a similar second chance at life?

The truth seems to have been that the authorities felt that the availability of a parachute might induce a pilot to jump prematurely when his aircraft was in difficulties. It was believed that somehow the parachute might impair the fighting spirit of pilots and cause them to abandon machines which might otherwise be capable of returning to base for repair – an illuminating reflection of the priorities placed on the relative value of the life of a pilot and the machine he was flying. In spite of the pressure from pilots, from the public and from the parachute manufacturers, the British authorities were able to resist issuing parachutes to their airmen until the mid-1920s.

They also had a somewhat cavalier attitude to strapping in – even to the provision of straps. Lieutenant Reynolds describes an incident when he was caught in a thunderstorm near Oxford in 1912. He had not bothered to strap himself in and his biplane was flipped upside down at 1,700 feet. 'I caught hold of the uprights at my side, for the next thing I realized I was lying in a heap on what is ordinarily the undersurface of the top plane [the upper wing].' His aircraft was then flipped back the right way up and he managed to hang on until he eventually crashed. He contrived to jump from his machine about ten feet from the ground – where he was met by two naked men who had been bathing nearby.

Reynolds survived. One who did not was Flight Sub Lieutenant Warneford, the officer who had been awarded the Victoria Cross for destroying a Zeppelin in the air. He was killed when the new Farman biplane in which he and an American newspaperman were flying pitched and bucked violently. The plane was so new that apparently it had no seat straps fitted; they both fell out and were killed. Warneford had won his Victoria Cross only ten days before.

Even those who had seat straps, and who used them, could not necessarily depend upon the straps to do what they were supposed to do. Graham Donald slipped out of his while he was doing a loop in his Royal Naval Air Service Sopwith Camel in 1917. He fell out at 6,000 feet. However, his Camel continued powering downwards for the remainder of the loop without its pilot and ended up underneath him as he plunged earthwards. Almost unbelievably he landed on the top wing of his aircraft having fallen 2,000 feet. Even more astonishingly, neither he nor his aircraft was damaged by their unlikely reunion. But he wasn't out of trouble yet. The aerodynamics of the Camel were not designed to cope with the pilot flopping onto the upper wing from a great height, and it quickly went into an upside-down spin. Somehow Donald succeeded in getting it the right way up again by poking his leg into the cockpit and pushing the control stick with his foot; hanging on for dear life, he managed to struggle into the cockpit, take control and land.[25] Shoulder straps, which retained the pilot more surely in his seat were brought in soon afterwards.

When one reads the accounts of the lives of these early military aviators it seems that life on an aviators' military camp on Salisbury Plain or at Eastchurch in 1911 must have been suffused with a very special atmosphere.

These young men, all volunteers for this hazardous duty of learning to fly, lived an intense, highly charged life. The elitism, the friendships, the rivalry, the risks, the achievements, the new records, the gaiety, the accidents, the injuries and death – all conspired to breed a body of men revelling in the insouciant knowledge that nobody had ever been there before. They were indeed 'those magnificent men and their flying machines'.

The first bomb dropped by an aircraft on a ship was during the Balkans War of 1913 when a Greek aircraft dropped some grenades on a Turkish battleship. Other fertile minds also turned to the possibility of bombing. In January 1912, a submariner called Lieutenant Williamson aired his ideas about how submarines might be destroyed by bombs which operated like depth charges, and work started in trying to turn his theories into reality. The great difficulty about dropping bombs with dependable accuracy is the need to calculate the numerous variables involved – the air speed, the ground speed, the height and aspect of the aircraft are the chief factors. Wind speed in relation to the target and wind resistance of the bomb will also affect the result. If the target is moving, these factors are multiplied. How to calculate all these in the air was the problem that faced the early bombers. Although bomb sights were developed and issued in due course, the results seem to have been indifferent.

Moreover, what would be the effect on the flight of a plane that had dropped a bomb? Samson conducted a number of hair-raising experiments to determine how low a plane could fly before it was affected by the bomb it had just dropped. An aircraft was flown over the sea at varying heights while explosive charges of up to 40lb weight were detonated electrically underneath it. From these tests it was concluded that an aircraft could drop a 100lb bomb containing 40lb of explosive from 300 feet without being in danger from the bomb.

Bombing in the Royal Flying Corps remained opportunistic and ad hoc well into 1915, and to begin with men simply dropped anything they could lay their hands on in the way of grenades, shells, darts and cans of petrol. When they were forced by circumstances to develop a bombing capability, they fumbled their way uncertainly into a science for which they were singularly ill-prepared.

On the other hand, Samson's men assumed bombing would soon be one of their main tasks in war. They understood that it was a specialist task which demanded its own doctrine and tactics. Appropriate aircraft and equipment would need to be developed, and pilots would need the right training. By 1914, the Royal Naval Air Service had taken some significant steps along that road. Work with radios also progressed to the point whereby aircraft were routinely carrying radios by the outbreak of war.

The Zeppelin threat remained the chief preoccupation for Royal Naval Air Service aviators and much thought was devoted to determining the best way to destroy them. Trials were conducted with an aircraft trailing a cable with an explosive grapnel attached to the end of it. More successful was the idea of dropping a series of small bombs or grenades with sensitive fuses on top of the Zeppelin. This presupposed that the aeroplane could get above the target, which, with the Zeppelin's ability to increase altitude rapidly, was by no means guaranteed. Therefore further trials were conducted whereby a Hales grenade was fired from a rifle into different types of cotton fabric. These were more successful. Work was also carried out with machine guns. Air trials using these methods against balloons were less than satisfactory because it was found that, without any way of observing the fall of shot, it was impossible to adjust fire onto the target. This remained a problem with all ground-to-air and air-to-air encounters until tracer rounds were developed and introduced during the war.

By the time the war started, the Royal Naval Air Service had been transformed. It had recovered from the *Mayfly* failure. As much by accident as than by intent, it had diverted the main thrust of its efforts towards the more fruitful heavier- rather than lighter-than-air flight. It had grown into a vibrant, adventurous organisation with diverse and improving capabilities. It had trained 100 pilots and had established a chain of seaplane and airship stations on the east coast. Thirty-nine aeroplanes and fifty-two seaplanes were in service, and a further forty-six were on order. It also had seven non-dirigible airships. The obsolete light cruiser HMS *Hermes* had been taken in hand as a seaplane carrier in 1912 and had been operating with the fleet since July 1913. She was in refit in August 1914 and was about to re-enter service even more capable than before. Three cross-Channel ferries, *Engadine*, *Riviera* and *Empress*, had either joined, or were about to join the Fleet as seaplane tenders. All the relevant air-related threats and the possibilities for offence and defence had been identified and the Service had advanced well along the road to producing men, equipment and tactics with which to counter them. From a standing start, well behind all the other major belligerents, the Royal Navy had built, in less than three years.[26] 'The largest, best organised and most experienced air arm of them all.'

Notes

1 Gordon, Andrew, *The Rules of the Game: Jutland and British Naval Command*, John Murray, 1996, p. 160.

2 Marder, Arthur J., *From Dreadnought to Scapa Flow*, OUP, 1961, p. 6, quoted by Richard Holmes in *In the Footsteps of Churchill*, BBC Books, 2005, p. 96.

3 See the works of Professors Andrew Lambert, John Beeler and Eric Grove.

4 Thompson, Julian, *The Imperial War Museum Book of the War at Sea 1914-1918*, Pan Books, 2005.

5 Marder, Arthur J., *From Dreadnought to Scapa Flow*, vol. I, *The Road to War 1904-1914*, OUP, 1961, p. 435, quoted by Julian Thompson in *The Imperial War Museum of the War at Sea 1914-1918*.

6 Craig, Gordon, *Germany 1866-1945*, OUP, 1978. p. 310.

7 Ibid., p. 309.

8 Gudehus, H.C. Gustav, *Personal Memoirs (1934)*, from the papers of Dr Timm Gudehus.

9 Raleigh, Walter, *Official History of the War: The War in the Air*, vol. I, OUP, 1922, p. 3.

10 Jones, Neville, *The Origins of Strategic Bombing*, William Kimber, 1973, p. 26.

11 Report of the Esher Committee, 28 January 1909, AIR1/2100,207/281, quoted by Neville Jones in *The Origins of Strategic Bombing*, p. 29.

12 Jones, Neville, *The Origins of Strategic Bombing*, William Kimber, 1973, p. 34.

13 Ibid., p. 74.

14 Raleigh, *Official History of the War: The War in the Air*, vol. I, p. 206.

15 Report of Technical Sub Committee of Committee of Imperial Defence, dated 17 February 1912, quoted by Neville Jones in *The Origins of Strategic Bombing*, p. 38.

16 Strachan, Hew (selected by), *Military Lives*, OUP, 2002, p. 451.

17 Raleigh, *Official History of the War: The War in the Air*, vol. I, p. 181.

18 Churchill, Winston, *The World Crisis 1911-1914*, Thornton Butterworth, 1923, p. 313.

19 Rimmel, Raymond, *Zeppelin! A Battle for Air Supremacy in World War One*, Conway Maritime Press, 1984, p. 69.

20 Raleigh, *Official History of the War: the War in the Air*, vol. I, p. 258, quoting the diary of Major Burke, a squadron commander of the RFC.

21 The author's father, who was aged eleven at the outbreak of war, remembered adults talking about the 'Zeppelin menace'.

22 Raleigh, *Official History of the War*, p. 205.

23 Begall, Sabine of the University of Duisberg-Essen, paper published in *Proceedings of the National Academy of Sciences* reported in *The Economist*, 30 August-5 September 2008, p. 84.

24 Strachan, *Military Lives*, p. 206.

25 Levine, Joshua, *On a Wing and a Prayer*, HarperCollins, 2008, p79.

26 Layman, R.D., *Naval Aviation in the First World War*, Chatham Publishing, 1996, p. 36.

Chapter 3

Düsseldorf – The First Raiders

If you go to a quiet field high above the modern, busy Channel port of Dover, close by the unnumbered road from the village of St Margaret's, you will find, by a gate into the field, a memorial commemorating the departure from that field of Numbers 2, 3, 4 and 5 Squadrons of the Royal Flying Corps to France between 13 and 15 August 1914. It is impossible not to be moved when pondering over what this simple stone signifies. The Italians had taken a small number of aircraft to Africa in the Somaliland expedition of 1912 and the Greeks had bombed Turkish ships in February 1913. But this was where, for the first time in history, an entire military air arm took to the air to go to war. The flight itself must have been a great adventure. Flying of any kind was barely out of its infancy. The Royal Flying Corps, formed in April 1912, was less than three years old. Although their brother officers in the Royal Naval Air Service had developed substantial experience flying over the sea, these soldiers would have been unusually brave – irrationally brave – men not to have been apprehensive at crossing such a large expanse of water. Louis Blériot, whose own memorial is barely a mile away, had achieved his cross-Channel aviation feat only five years before.

Flying in peacetime was dangerous enough. Of those men who took to the air in the early days, only about half of them had been able to control the inexorable unforgiving forces of gravity without losing their lives. The squadrons had already suffered two fatal casualties in a crash as they had gathered from their base airfields to concentrate at Dover. Now the German forces were going to join the forces of gravity to conspire against them. To fly to war across the Channel was to launch into a great unknown. Their logistics and repair unit, the Aircraft Park, went by sea. It too was to enounter its own unknowns. On its arrival unannounced at Boulogne, the baffled harbour officer was moved to send a plaintive signal: 'An unnumbered unit without aeroplanes which calls itself an Aircraft Park has arrived. What are we to do with it?'

But they all made it across the water, heading for Amiens. A couple of the machines were damaged when they landed in a ploughed field, and one pilot rejoined his squadron at Amiens a week late having been arrested by the French authorities after crash landing near Boulogne. But they all made it. Before they got anywhere near the Germans, they were fired at by the French and the British, so they spent all night one night painting Union Jacks on the underside of their wings. They sustained their first fatal casualties overseas in a crash on the 16th and they were in the thick of the action with the British Expeditionary Force within another week. Astonishingly, most of those who flew across the Channel in August 1914 were to survive the War. One who did not, Captain Anketell Read, won a posthumous Victoria Cross – but not as an airman. He was killed at the Battle of Loos serving with his parent infantry battalion, having reverted to terrestial warfare.[1]

Meanwhile, the Royal Naval Air Service enjoyed an even less orthodox commencement to hostilties. For them the first priority was to ensure that the British Expeditionary Force crossed the Channel without interference from the enemy, and this was achieved under the aegis of non-rigid airship patrols. Other elements of the Service were parcelled out in their air stations dedicated to defensive coastal patrols. But it was not long before minds were turned to devising ways of going over to the offensive. Damage to the locks on the Kiel Canal, which would have restricted the movements of vessels along that strategic waterway, or to the docks at Kiel, were tempting possibilities. And the German High Seas Fleet, lying unscathed at its base at Wilhelmshaven, was for many a floating reproach to the Royal Navy's impotence. But its airships, being smaller and less capable than the dirigible Zeppelins, did not have the range and carrying capacity to threaten the German coast. Its seaplanes were still in the experimental stage and, even though bomb sights and bomb racks were being developed, it was as yet impossible to take off in a seaplane from the water with a bomb load on board. But active minds were working on these problems and, before the year was out, the first carrier air strike would be mounted on the base of the German fleet. Meanwhile, the question was: how to get within striking range of the enemy's ships and vital infrastructures? The answer was, of course, to set up a base in Belgium.

Charles Samson, now sporting the Royal Naval Air Service rank of wing commander, and nine of his pilots, flew an assortment of aeroplanes from Eastchurch to Ostend on 27 August to support the Royal Marines defending that Channel port. They flew with Union Jacks lashed to one of the wing strutts and each pilot was encircled with a couple of bicycle tyres by way of a lifebelt. Another three pilots went across by airship. Again, almost all of these men would survive the war, and one, Richard Bell-Davies, would also win a Victoria Cross. Only Flight Lieutenant Charles Beevor, who died on 5 November 1914, and one of the balloon pilots, Wing

Commander Neville Usborne, who died on 21 February 1916, are recorded on the Commonwealth War Graves website. Two of Samson's brothers, Felix and Bill, both also pilots, joined them in Belgium soon after their arrival.

Landing on the racecourse at Ostend, Samson's pilots too were shot at by friendly forces long before they were shot at by Germans, this time by Royal Marines. The sentry who stalked Samson on his arrival was very disappointed to find his quarry was a Royal Navy officer. While in Ostend, they cruised around Belgium in aeroplanes and motor cars, enjoying the adulation of the Belgians who thought they were going to defend them against the Germans. However, it was very soon clear that the defence of Ostend was not a realistic proposition. They had been on the Continent for only three days before they were ordered home. Crestfallen, they set off for Dunkirk for the journey back to England but fortunately one of them crashed, thus giving Samson enough leeway to delay the journey back across the Channel in the hope that a pretext might be found for them to stay on the Continent. In response to the demands for their return, and for explanations for the delay, the 'fog in channel' gambit was used with boyish, hopeful glee. And it worked; just long enough for the plan to change yet again. On 1 September, the order to come home was rescinded.

Reading accounts of those days one is struck with the air of confusion and disorder that attended the opening moments of the war for the Royal Naval Air Service. Order, counter-order, disorder: this is usually a recipe for confusion, despondency and recrimination, but not for Wing Commander Charles Samson. For him it offered abundant opportunities to make his own mark and to do his own thing. One also senses that he used his friendship with the First Lord of the Admiralty freely and shamelessly.

Churchill, whether he shared the public's hysteria or not, as a shrewd politician he was certainly sensitive to the Zeppelin threat. The Zeppelin's principal role was maritime reconnaissance and as the political head of the Navy, and one who frequently behaved as if he were its operational head, he was anxious to negate the significant advantage they gave to the German Navy. Moreover, the Army were responsible for the aerial defence of the United Kingdom, but Churchill had noted that, in the years before the war, they had barely paid even lip service to this commitment. It was naval installations, ports, oil dumps etc. which were most at risk from aerial attack and so he had, bit by bit, equipped the Royal Naval Air Service so that it could do something about making aerial defence a reality if required. When the entire force of available Army aeroplanes deployed to France to support the British Expeditionary Force, the situation that he foresaw came about. On 3 September, Lord Kitchener, as political head of the Army, asked him if the Navy could take over the responsibility for aerial defence and he agreed.

In 1914, the Germans had aircraft capable of bombing Britain, but only from Calais. Since they never captured Calais, they were forced to base these machines in Ostend which put Britain out of their range. But the Zeppelin was not so constrained. Churchill, while he did not consider that attack from the air could yet produce a decisive result, was conscious of the likelihood of a public outcry if such an attack came.[2] At the end of 1914, he was sufficiently concerned to forward a paper to his fellow Cabinet members reporting that twenty Zeppelins were capable of reaching London, each carrying a ton or so of high explosive. British defensive forces would be powerless to stop them, he reported, and: 'The unavenged destruction of non-combatant life may therefore be very considerable.' Churchill confined himself to setting out what he believed to be the facts. Not so the First Sea Lord, the reappointed Admiral Jackie Fisher, who feared that H.G. Wells's prediction would come true on his watch and that he would be held accountable. A number of German citizens either living in Britain, or trapped by the war while passing through, had been interned at the beginning of the war. Fisher urged that a substantial portion of them should be taken to one side and the intention be declared of executing them one by one for each British civilian killed by German bombs – he even threatened to resign if this were not done. Churchill deftly brushed aside this hysterical nonsense with some tact and skill – not to mention humanity. Fisher stayed at his post and the interned Germans remained unmolested.[3]

But in spite of the scepticism that he declared after the war, Churchill had every good reason to seek out whatever means he could to destroy Zeppelins. He knew they were very prickly porcupines for the aircraft of the day to deal with, so he decided to strike at Zeppelin sheds wherever they could be found and reached. He argued that since 'it was impossible to provide effectively by means of passive defences for every vulnerable point liable to aircraft attack', the natural approach 'was to attack the sheds and bases of the enemy's aircraft'.

> It was easy to order the necessary guns, searchlights etc and set on foot the organisation which should employ them. But it was no use sitting down for a year while these preparations were completing. Only offensive action could help us. I decided immediately to strike, by bombing from aeroplanes the Zeppelin sheds wherever these gigantic structures could be found in Germany, and secondly to prevent the erection of any new Zeppelin sheds in the conquered parts of Belgium or France. Here again the policy was right. Our resources were, however, feeble and slender. Compared to the developments at the end of the war they were puny. Still, they were

all we had, and all that our knowledge of aviation at that time could bestow. Deficiencies in material had to be made good by daring.[4]

Consequently, on 1 September, he wrote to Sueter:

> The largest possible force of naval aeroplanes should be stationed in Calais or Dunkirk. ... it is extremely probable that the Germans will attempt to attack London ... by Zeppelin airships. ... the proper defence is a thorough and continual search of the country for 70 to 100 miles inland with a view to marking down any temporary airship bases ... should such be located they should be immediately attacked.

When possible, attacks were to be made on the two sheds at Düsseldorf and Cologne.

On the same day, Samson and his force were ordered to remain at Dunkirk, and a signal was sent from Churchill's Admiralty to the French authorities seeking approval for them to have a roving commission 'to deny the use of territory within a hundred miles of Dunkirk to German Zeppelins, and to attack by aeroplanes all airships found replenishing there'. In order that they should have a good radius of action, the Royal Naval Air Service should be able to establish temporary forward operating bases 40 to 50 miles inland. There then followed a series of bold adventures, and alarums and excursions more redolent of the Long Range Desert Group of the Second World War than the lethal stasis that beset the First. And to begin with at least, it had very little to do with countering the Zeppelin threat.

The German Army, in pursuance of the plan devised by the late Field Marshal von Schlieffen, had swept through Belgium and northern France in a grand wheeling hook designed to circle round to the south and west of Paris. The outer radius of this wheeling movement was General von Kluck's First Army. The fighting head of this Army had passed through Belgium and was by now engaged further south between the Somme and the Marne rivers. Soon, the Germans would pull their punches and, instead of circling west round Paris, von Kluck and the rest of the German Army would be stopped north of Paris on the Marne River. Meanwhile von Kluck's lines of communication were exposed to attack from his right flank, on which sat the ports of Calais, Dunkirk, Ostend and Antwerp.

Samson as usual made much of the latitude of his brief. Nominally in support of the French local forces, the Royal Naval Air Service then started to operate more like Boer commandos rather than nascent naval aviators. With the appropriately named Major Charles Risk of the the Royal Marines Light Infantry in command, taking their own cars – one of them had a Rolls Royce – they borrowed lorries, machine guns and more cars, and set off like naughty boys playing at pirates and buccaneers. Using aeroplanes for reconnaissance and motor cars to strike, they raided the German First Army's lines of communications as the Marne battle further south was getting into full swing. They bombed motor cars and formations of marching German soldiers. They skirmished with the occasional German patrol and when the German Army left Lille, Samson occupied and 'liberated' it with his motley troop. They then contrived to armour their cars with the assistance of the Dunkirk shipyard, thus predating the advent of the tank in battle by nearly two years. By the end of 1914, their armoured cars had machine guns mounted in turrets and are recognisably the progenitors of all armoured cars ever since.

Credit for inventing the tank has a number of claimants. Someone in Samson's squadron, perhaps Samson himself, must have twigged to the possibilities of bolting metal sheets onto the sides of their cars. It wasn't long before they routinely carried planks to help get them across rough ground. Colonel Swinton of the Royal Engineers has been credited with taking the next step and devising the tracked armoured vehicle. However Murray Sueter maintained that this was his idea and certainly the recognisable prototypes of what became a tracked armoured vehicle were first produced and tested under his aegis. On 16 February 1915, Sueter demonstrated his caterpillar idea to Winston Churchill on Horse Guards Parade – appropriately enough, as the trial version was drawn by a horse, it having no self-motive power.[5] Churchill implied that he had had a hand in the new invention.[6] The probable truth is that the tank was the child of no one man's brain, but the Royal Naval Air Service provided the bureaucratic space for the development of a weapon not mainstream to either the Admiralty or the War Office. What is beyond doubt is that in the autumn of 1914, the Royal Naval Air Service was conducting mobile armoured land and air operations in a fashion recognisably similar to the way armoured land and air operations were conducted in the Second World War, and in every other conventional war since.

Churchill, sensing that they might be on to something good, bought as many Rolls Royces as he could lay his hands on, had them armoured and sent them to join Samson, together with 250 Royal Marines. Like a good guerilla leader, Samson knew that he couldn't take the Germans on in strength, but so long as they were distracted elsewhere, he could be more than a nuisance in their rear. With his secure base in Dunkirk, and temporary forward operating bases inland as required, and using his aeroplanes for reconnaissance and his cars for offensive mobility, he was able to avoid being caught in pitched battles by superior forces. This sporting banditry of the Royal Naval Air Service had very little tangible result in the long run – there simply were not enough of them – and the course of the war was hardly diverted by their escapades. But their encounters with horse-mounted Uhlans are redolent of the stories, or myths, of German panzers encountering Polish horse-mounted cavalry at the beginning of the next world conflict, with similar results. As well as pioneering maritime aviation and strategic bombing, the Royal Navy can also claim a first in mobile armoured strike and reconnaissance operations, and in active co-operation between air and armoured land forces.

The original aim of keeping Samson and his men at Dunkirk, namely to counter the Zeppelin threat, had not been forgotten. One reason why the Royal Naval Air Service had resorted to driving around in cars was because they did not have enough aircraft to cover all the ground. They had also organised a telephone service to give early warning of approaching Zeppelins. When Churchill gave Samson instructions to destroy the Zeppelin sheds at Cologne and Düsseldorf, three aircraft, a Farman, a BE and a Bristol, were specially detached from Dunkirk and sent to Ostend on 3 September under the supervision of Major Eugene Gerrard of the Royal Marine Light Infantry.

Antwerp was still in Allied hands and this seemed the most convenient mounting base for the first strategic air raid in history, so Gerrard went up the road to Antwerp to scout out a suitable forward mounting airfield, and to make the necessary arrangements. The aircraft meanwhile remained at Ostend secured with pegs and guys in the lee of some sand dunes. Then, during the night of 12/13 September, a furious wind gusting to 70 mph hit them and ripped out their moorings from the sand. The sentry gave the alarm and all the officers and men who were sleeping in a lean-to within 100 yards turned out instantly. But it was all over in less than a minute and the gale cart-wheeled the fragile aircraft along the foreshore, reducing them to matchwood. Two Belgian machines were also destroyed.

Unsurprisingly, in light of the scale of subsequent destruction and loss of life, history contents itself with simply relating these bare facts. But it takes only a little pause for thought to imagine Eugene Gerrard's horror when he learned that these scarce and precious aircraft, which had been placed in his charge for him to lead this ground-breaking air raid, had been hurled several hundred yards along the sand dunes to complete destruction. Doubtless he wondered whether his career was about to share the fate of his planes. Happily it did not. Meanwhile, he and his party returned crestfallen and aircraftless to Dunkirk, and the Zeppelin sheds remained unassailed.

The pressure to conduct a successful attack on the Zeppelin sheds was more intense than ever and Samson scraped together four more aircraft out of his meagre force. Again Antwerp, which it was hoped at that stage could be retained by the Allies, was to be the mounting base. However, it was

Map 1 - Antwerp to Dusseldorf, September to October 1914.

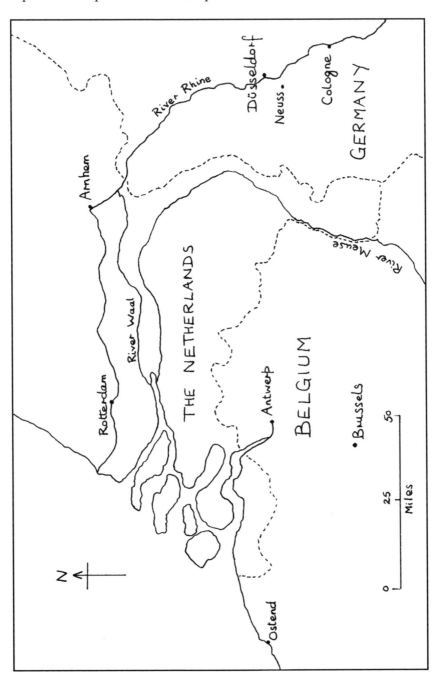

clear that the aircraft would not have the range to fly to the targets and return without refuelling. So an arrangement was made with a Belgian ground unit to set up a forward refuelling base with cars some 50 miles east of Antwerp.

On 22 September, Major Eugene Gerrard RMLI, Lieutenant Charles Collet of the Royal Marine Artillery, Flight Lieutenant Reginald Marix and Squadron Commander Spenser Grey all took off shortly after daylight. Spenser Grey was famous in naval circles before the war for commuting daily to work in his own seaplane. He used to park it overnight by South Parade Pier near his home in Southsea and fly 10 miles across Southampton Water to the naval air station at Calshot, thereby saving himself a 40-mile trip by road. He carried a passenger, Flight Lieutenant Newton-Clare. Gerrard and Collet, the Royal Marines pilots, were to hit the sheds at Düsseldorf; Marix and Grey were to do the same at Cologne. The strikes were timed to be simultaneous.

They set off in good weather, but by the time they crossed the River Meuse it was misty and cloudy. The Cologne pair tried to get down below the cloud but nearly crashed into the ground in the attempt – it was 100 per cent cloud cover down to ground level. One of the Düsseldorf pair, Collet, found a gap in the clouds. He glided down from 6,000 feet, much of it through thick mist, until he suddenly saw the shed a quarter of a mile away. He dropped his two 20lb Hales bombs at 400 feet. In fact they only weighed 18.5lb, of which a mere 4.5lb comprised explosive charge. The fuses were armed by means of rotating propeller-like vanes extending out from the tail fin. The air rushing through the vanes turned it, but if it was dropped at too low an altitude, then it did not turn the required number of revolutions. It is likely that this is what happened to Collet's bombs, which either didn't explode or he missed the shed, because there was no significant result. Contemporary reports suggest that some men were killed and some windows were blown out. Collet's aircraft was hit by ground fire but its performance was not impaired. All the aircraft found the refuelling point in the field on the way back, topped up with fuel and recovered successfully to Antwerp. One of Grey's bombs was found to be missing on his return. He had no idea where it had fallen off but was concerned that it might have dropped on neutral Holland.

Disappointing though the results may have been, this was proof that it could be done. It was also a shock for the Germans to have the vulnerability of their airships thus demonstrated, for they had not believed it was possible to fly such a distance with bombs, attack their sheds and return. Collet was awarded the Distinguished Service Order for this exploit, the first ever strategic bombing air raid in history.

The weather remained unfavourable for the next week, there were various technical delays and, by the beginning of October, the military situation in Antwerp had deteriorated quite markedly. But it was still hoped to mount the next raid from Antwerp. Nowhere else was within range of the Zeppelin sheds and, if this opportunity were not taken, it would disappear for ever. The increasing presence of the German Army in strength ruled out any possibility of forward refuelling bases so two pilots, Marix and Spenser Grey, arranged to have an extra fuel tank fitted to their aircraft.

The aircraft they were flying were Sopwith Tabloids. The Tabloid was a single seater biplane – although there were early twin-seater versions with the pilot and the passenger sitting side by side – and was a land adaptation of a seaplane which had been built for racing. It had a 25-foot wing span and had warping wings rather than ailerons, and, with a speed of 92 mph, it was the fastest biplane in the world in 1913 with an exceptional rate of climb of 1,200 feet per minute. Again, the engine was a seven-cylinder Gnome 80 horse power rotary engine inside a metal cowling with cooling slits.

A rotary engine should not be confused with a radial engine. In both types, the cylinders were configured radially, rather like the spokes of a wheel. However, the radial engine operated in the conventional way with a revolving crankshaft. A rotary engine, instead of driving a propeller on a revolving shaft, itself revolved at high speed together with the propeller around a fixed crankshaft. The Gnome engine ran on petrol, with castor oil added as a lubricant, and much of the oil spewed out with the exhaust. To start the engine, it was turned over by hand by a ground crewman until all the cylinders were well primed with fuel. When the propeller was swung to ignite the engine, it was not unusual for excess fuel to burst into flames and, if the excess spilled over onto grass under the machine, things could become interesting indeed. When the engine was running, the general effect was like that of a damp Catherine wheel firework. When sitting behind this engine, it was not unusual for the face of the pilot to be sprayed with oil – some pilots believed that the castor oil had a lubricating effect on their bowels as well as their engines.

The advantage of a rotary engine was that it required no radiator system and no flywheel. Therefore, being lighter than a liquid-cooled engine, it had a higher ratio of power to weight than conventional engines. Moreover, unlike many other early engines, it did not suffer from excessive vibration. The disadvantages – apart from its effect on the pilots' bowels and its tendency to burst into flames when starting – were that it had a high rate of fuel consumption and it was of greater complexity than conventional engines. This meant that it required more maintenance time and could be temperamental. No two engines seemed to be quite alike and all demanded constant care and attention. The early rotaries had only two speeds: full speed and stop; the speed could not be adjusted. Moreover, the large lump of metal rotating clockwise at speed at the front of the aircraft had a gyroscopic effect. This meant that turning the aircraft to the left tended to lift the nose, while turning to the right tended to drop it.[7] This had important implications for fighter aircraft like the Sopwith Camel because it made them especially nimble on right turns. But it could also mean that an enemy pilot who spotted that his adversary was powered by a rotary engine might guess and anticipate which way he would turn. To counter this, some engines were adapted so that they rotated the other way (i.e. anti-clockwise). Rotary engines also had a tendency to shed cylinders. Taken altogether, while one sat behind a halo of flames, exhaust gas and castor oil fumes, a rotary engine could make for adventurous and unpredictable flying.

The two Sopwith aircraft that Reginald Marix and Spenser Grey were flying were destined for short but eventful careers with the Royal Navy. They had acquired them in a somewhat unorthodox way. One morning in early September 1914, Marix was at Eastchurch when he received a phone call from Grey, who was ringing from Churchill's official residence in London, Admiralty House. Marix should drop everything, get himself into London and join him as soon as possible. Marix was deep inside a Gnome engine at the time and was covered in oil but, sensing the urgency in Spenser Grey's voice, he didn't bother to clean himself up. He drove to London in an open-topped staff car, thereby getting even dirtier, and arrived at Admiralty House shortly after lunch. He was ushered into a dining room where Churchill, Grey and 'an old man with grizzled white hair, dressed in an old fashioned black frock coat but wearing what looked like a petty officer's India rubber or celluloid collar and a narrow bright red tie'[8] were finishing lunch. Churchill welcomed Marix and offered him coffee and brandy in a balloon glass. A discussion on how best to attack the Zeppelin sheds at Cologne and Düsseldorf then ensued. How could it be done with the aircraft available at the time? During the course of the discussion, it dawned on Marix that the old man with the grizzled white hair, whom he had hitherto rather ignored, was Admiral Jackie Fisher. Fisher did not return to his former post of First Sea Lord until over two months later but he was in the habit of visiting the Admiralty from time to time. Presumably this was one of those occasions. In any event, Marix rather belatedly started inserting 'sir' into his replies to Fisher's questions.

Churchill then told them of two Sopwith Tabloid aircraft which the Royal Flying Corps had sent to the Aircraft Factory at Farnborough for trials. At that stage, while it was Royal Flying Corps policy to take aircraft only from Farnborough, the Royal Naval Air Service was happy to deal directly with civilian aircraft manufacturers. Quite how the Royal Flying

Corps had come by the two Sopwiths is not clear, but their pilots plainly had had their reservations with them. These probably arose out of inexperience because the Tabloid proved to be an excellent aircraft in the hands of experienced pilots. But Farnborough evidently shared these reservations and had declared them to be unsafe. They were now sitting there for the taking. Would Grey and Marix like to go to Farnborough and try them out? Yes, of course they would. The meeting over, Marix and Grey were then introduced to Mrs Clementine Churchill, Marix more conscious than ever of his filthy, oily hands.

Off they went to Farnborough the following day where they were warned that the planes were dangerous. They were unstable when flown at full speed. Because the Gnome engine only flew at one speed, namely full speed, this presented a problem. The suggested solution was either to climb or glide, but always to avoid flying level. Gliding necessitated shutting the engine off. This seems to have been standard practice with the Gnome, but it was always a matter of some uncertainty whether it would start again when required and one had to make sure one had enough speed and height to give oneself the best possible chance. And by the way, they should not leave the vicinity of the airfield as, in the event of engine failure, they were impossible to land in a field. Marix and Grey took off, having previously agreed that, if they were happy, they would fly straight to Eastchurch without any further formality. They made a few circuits. Marix found the aircraft lighter on the controls than any other aircraft he had flown but otherwise he felt it flew well. Grey evidently shared his satisfaction. After a short while they waved at each other 'and that was the last Farnborough saw of the two Tabloids'.[9]

But Marix was to find that the advice they had been given at Farnborough about the difficulty of landing was not entirely misguided – he broke the undercarriage and lower wing of his plane on arrival at Eastchurch.

By 7 October, Antwerp was under attack from artillery, with shells passing over the airfield at Wilryck to the south of the city on their way to the town. The Royal Naval Air Service aircraft were parked out in the middle of the airfield in the hope that they would not be damaged if the aircraft sheds were hit. Churchill himself had turned up on 3 October in the hope of bolstering the Belgian authorities' will to defend the town. But by now it was clear that the town would fall into German hands any day and it looked increasingly as if it would be too late to conduct a raid. Then, on 8 October, the weather cleared. Would there be time to mount another strike at the Zeppelins? Reginald Marix and Spenser Grey went into town to find Churchill and get his permission. Grey knew Churchill well. As well as having been included by Churchill in discussions about what to do about

Zeppelins, Grey had taken him up in his aeroplane at Eastchurch on several occasions[10] and had given him flying lessons. The two officers found Churchill in his headquarters at the Hotel St Antoine, where they told him that they were ready and willing to go on the raid. Churchill said that it was now too late – Antwerp was to be evacuated that day and the Germans could arrive at any time. The Royal Naval Air Service should now abandon Wilryck and return to Ostend or Dunkirk. That was that.

According to Marix,[11] Churchill then retired to the lavatory. Grey followed him, pleading with him through the lavatory door, maintaining that, if they went now, they would still have time to complete the raid, return and get out. Probably as much to get rid of him as anything else, an exasperated Churchill finally gave his assent. Marix and Grey sped back to the airfield and took off in the early afternoon, Marix bound for Düsseldorf and Grey for Cologne. It was 110 miles to the targets. Each plane had two 20lb Hales bombs fixed to a bomb rack under the fuselage. They were released by pulling on two toggles connected by wires to the split pins holding the bombs on the rack. Neither pilot had bomb sights.

Spenser Grey once again encountered thick mist over Cologne. He circled the city but could not find the Zeppelin shed so he dropped his bombs instead on the main railway station where he saw many trains drawn up. No damage was reported. Reginald Marix on the other hand had a straightforward flight. The shed was not where he expected it, but he found it nevertheless. He was at 3,000 feet when inaccurate anti-aircraft fire came his way so it was clear he had lost any element of surprise. Moreover, the Germans had beefed up their defences since Charles Collet's raid two weeks before. With no bomb sight, the only way to try and ensure the bomb went anywhere near the target was to dive towards it and release as close as possible; but, remembering Collet, not so close that the bombs would not have time to fuse. Marix started his dive towards the shed. There was a risk when diving with a rotary engine that it would push the revolutions up beyond what it could endure. On the other hand, Marix was anxious not to be caught near the ground trying to start his engine, or, having started it, found waiting for it to pick up power. So he did not switch his engine off. Instead, he kept it going at full power because there was no way of adjusting it. The risk paid off and his engine withstood the strain. At 500 feet, he pulled his toggles, released his bombs one after the other and pulled out of the dive. This time the bombs did explode. He saw the flashes of machine guns firing up at him as he pulled out, but as he looked over his shoulder, he saw enormous sheets of flame pouring out of the Zeppelin shed behind him. But his plane had been hit, his rudder bar was jammed and he was heading away from home further into Germany. Turning his plane by warping his wings, he managed to set a course for Antwerp.

Marix was flying by compass, but the wind blew him off course to the north. By the time he realised this, he was getting low on fuel. As he had already discovered, the Tabloid was not an easy plane to land in an emergency at the best of times. With a damaged rudder, it would not be any easier. So he looked for a suitable field while he still had the choice of landing grounds. He got down safely and found that, although his plane had been hit about thirty times, it was still airworthy. He also found a hole through the peak of his uniform cap which had been hanging round his neck. He hoped to get into Antwerp and return the following day with a mechanic and some fuel.

Some Belgian gendarmes placed a guard on his plane and helped him to a nearby railway station where he hitched a ride on the footplate of a train which was going into Antwerp to evacuate refugees. This took him to within 5 miles of the city where he 'commandeered' a bicycle. After further adventures, which included slinging his bike on his back and climbing along the outside of the parapet of a blocked bridge, he arrived back at the Hotel St Antoine that night. The hotel and Antwerp were deserted and some houses were on fire. Churchill and, it appeared, everybody else, had gone. He found a caretaker in the hotel who provided some food and drink. Some Belgian soldiers then drove him out to the airfield where he found Spenser Grey and Sidney Sippe about to depart in lorries. All serviceable aircraft had already been flown out. It was by now dark and Marix joined the party which headed west in a lorry, competing for road space with the sad sight of women, children and old men pushing their belongings in wheelbarrows. He got to Ghent soon after dawn and thenceforth to Ostend. He never heard what happened to his aircraft. Both it and Grey's were abandoned in the retreat from Antwerp.

The elation on the Allied side was considerable. At last a successful strike had been made on the dreaded Zeppelins on Germany's home ground. The notion that a heavier-than-air machine might have the flexibility, lift capability and range to destroy a dirigible in its base was both novel and exciting. It was also something of a consolation, however small, for the loss of Antwerp, and a lift for the Royal Navy which felt it had been in the shadow of the Army which seemed to have hogged the limelight since the start of the war.

Both Reginald Marix and Spenser Grey were awarded the Distinguished Service Order. The press had a field day. Much speculation took place over what had been destroyed. Was it one Zeppelin, or was it more? The shed, which Marix also destroyed, appeared to be big enough to take more than one airship. The *Illustrated War News* of 14 October 1914 hungrily grabbed this notion and actually published a photograph of the shed, with a second dirigible drawn into the picture, purporting to illustrate how it might have contained another machine. Rumours arrived from neutral Holland that there might even have been three airships in the shed. Notwithstanding the newspapermen's fantasy, Marix had in fact destroyed one new army Zeppelin.

This was a significant enough blow. The German Army had had six Zeppelins at the outbreak of war. Two had been destroyed while conducting low-level daylight reconnaissance over enemy troops. A third had been riddled by friendly fire and had drifted out of control before finally being brought down by the French. A fourth had been lost elsewhere and Marix had now destroyed a fifth.

In German circles there was talk of treachery. Someone must have passed information to the British. Some clerks in the American embassy were arrested. But there was no treachery. It simply seemed obvious to the aviators that if you saw a Zeppelin shed, then there was a fair chance that there might be a Zeppelin in it. As Marix said, 'I had received no information. It was just luck that a Zepp was in the shed.'

The raids on both cities had at least one unforeseen side effect. Some days afterwards, a German aircraft was flying over Neuss near Düsseldorf and not far from Cologne. Perhaps overly sensitive in the aftermath of Grey's and Marix's raid, 'It was taken for an English one and the whole population fired at it bringing it down.'[12] The two unfortunate German aviators were killed.

But there was another intangible result of the raid – intangible and unseen, but no less significant for all that. The assault was not simply an attack on the Zeppelin, it was also an attack upon the Zeppelin myth. The Zeppelin had captured the imaginations of both Germans and British in opposite ways. The success of this raid reduced the potency of the Zeppelin bogey in the minds of the British, and induced doubt and anxiety for their precious totem in the minds of the Germans. The raid demonstrated to the Germans that their Zeppelin bases could no longer be regarded as safe – they would now have to deploy anti-aircraft measures at all Zeppelin installations within range of British aircraft. Notwithstanding that by capturing Antwerp, the Germans had put most of their installations out of range of British bases, they were in no doubt that sooner or later the British would find a means of trying again.

Little did Reginald Marix realise that, within a mere thirty years, his successors would deliver, from one aircraft, a single projectile weighing a thousand times the weight of one of his bombs. And that before his career as an airman was over, a nightmare which not even H.G. Wells had dreamt of would come to pass: with one single piece of ordnance dropped from the air, men would reduce an entire city to a chaotic, shattered, smouldering hell.

Notes

1 In Raleigh, Walter, *Official History of the War: The War in the Air*, vol. I, OUP, 1922, pp. 288-92. The author lists the names of those who deployed to war with 2, 3, 4 and 5 Squadrons. Out of eighty or so names who probably flew rather than sailed, only four are listed in the Commonwealth War Graves Commission website as casualties of the war.

2 Public Record Office paper CAB 37/121/123.

3 Churchill, Winston, *The World Crisis 1915*, Charles Scribner's Sons, 1929, pp. 51-3.

4 Churchill, Winston, *The World Crisis 1912-1914*, Thornton Butterworth, 1923, p. 314.

5 Sueter, Murray, *The Evolution of the Tank*, Hutchinson, 1937, p. 65.

6 Churchill, *The World Crisis 1912-1914*, p. 319.

7 It has been said that this tendency, caused by the rotary engine, is the reason why the island or the superstructure of the aircraft carrier was first placed on the starboard side of the flight deck. A pilot in difficulties and needing to abort on landing would want to turn up and away from such an obstacle rather than down and towards it.

8 Lea, John, *Reggie: The Life of Air Marshal R.L.G. Marix CBE DSO*, Pentland Press, 1994, p. 23.

9 Ibid., p. 24.

10 Turner, Charles, *The Od Flying Days*, Ayer Publishing, 1972, p. 21. According to Turner, Grey also too Clementine Churchill up, which may have had something to do with her lack of enthusiasm for Churchill's flying ambitions.

11 Lea, *Reggie*, p. 27.

12 Air Ministry Paper AIR 1/629/17/122/4 at Public Record Office, Kew.

Chapter 4

Friedrichshafen –
The Flatpack Bombers

With a whiff of cowardice and incompetence in the air, the Royal Navy had had a shaky start to the First World War.

Britain had declared war on Germany on 4 August 1914, but it was by no means certain that the Turks would join hostilities, and if so, on which side. This was of some importance because Turkey controlled the sea route to Russia through the Bosphorous and the Black Sea, and Russia was on the Allied side. Turkey had ordered two dreadnought battleships from British yards and these ships were all but ready to be delivered when war broke out. Germany, however, had done much to modernise the Turkish Army and her political influence with the government was strong. On 2 August, Britain learned that Turkey was likely to ally herself with Germany against Russia, and that the Turks proposed to send one of their new British-built battleships to a German port. This was more than Churchill could accept and so he requisitioned both new ships for the Royal Navy the following day. Had he at the same time offered the Turks compensation for their lost ships, he might have helped to mitigate the predictable righteous indignation with which the Turks reacted. But he did not. Turkey would probably have entered the war on the German side in any case, but this peremptory move made more certain that she would do so sooner rather than later.

Meanwhile, two German warships, the modern battlecruiser SMS *Goeben* and the light cruiser SMS *Breslau* were in the Mediterranean presenting a potential threat to Allied convoys. As Britain declared war on Germany, these two ships were ordered to sail to Istanbul. The Royal Navy tried to catch them and sink them before they could get there but, through a combination of indecision, faint hearts and back-seat driving by both Churchill and the admiral in command in the Mediterranean, they escaped unscathed. There also occurred a classic manifestation of the Royal Navy's most serious systemic problem. One of the Royal Navy's leading technologists, Captain Fawcett Wray, persuaded his commander, Rear

Admiral Ernest Troubridge, that the *Goeben* could clearly outfight his own cruisers – on paper. If he were to fight them in the face of this advice, Troubridge could only be seeking personal glory in a hopeless cause. Science won the argument and the Royal Navy lost the chance to sink the *Goeben* – and some of its own warrior reputation besides. The hapless Troubridge was court-martialled. Jackie Fisher wanted him shot for cowardice. But the real problems were systemic rather than attributable to one individual and Troubridge was acquitted, but it was a deeply humiliating start to hostilities for the Navy.

Two days after declaring war, Britain lost her first warship, the cruiser *Amphion*, which struck a mine off the Thames estuary drowning 132 sailors. However, at the end of that month, on 28 August, a cruiser squadron backed up by Admiral Beatty's battlecruisers encountered German cruisers near the German island of Heligoland. Three German light cruisers were destroyed and some 1,200 German sailors were lost in return for some damage to the British cruiser *Arethusa* and the loss of thirty-five sailors. What was not known at the time was that this battle, fought in the German Navy's back yard, served to make the Kaiser and the German High Command extra cautious about deploying their capital ships into the North Sea. For the British, it was a welcome victory after the fiasco in the Mediterranean, but nevertheless it was something of an anti-climax in view of the fact that they were really trying to entice some bigger fry to sea.

On 3 September, the torpedo gunboat *Speedy* was lost to a mine in the North Sea off the River Humber, on 5 September the cruiser *Pathfinder* went down to a submarine attack off the River Forth taking 250 men with her, and on 22 September three elderly cruisers, *Aboukir*, *Cressy* and *Hogue*, were torpedoed by a submarine off the Dutch coast and sank in quick succession. These three cruisers, which were referred to in some quarters as the 'live bait squadron', were needlessly exposed to danger and should not have been where they were. Nearly 1,500 sailors were lost.

Then, in the Indian Ocean, from 14 September over the next seventy days, the German cruiser SMS *Emden*, as well as bombarding Madras and Penang, captured or sank twenty-three Allied merchant vessels, plus a Russian and a French cruiser. She was finally caught and destroyed on 9 November by HMAS *Sydney* at the Cocos Islands. However *Emden*, in her short war cruise, had twisted the nose of the Royal Navy in a part of the world which was widely seen as a British lake.

On 20 September, the cruiser HMS *Pegasus*, while cleaning her boilers at sea, was sunk by gunfire by the German cruiser SMS *Königsberg* off the coast of Zanzibar. *Königsberg* then disappeared up the Rufiji River and defied the attempts of the Royal Navy to destroy her until July the following year. Meanwhile she forced the British to commit seven warships to ensure she didn't break out.

Then on 9 October, Antwerp fell to the German Army. The Marne battle had by now been lost by the Germans and the 'race to the sea' was on. The war of movement would continue until both sides squared up opposite each other across a line stretching from the Belgian coast to Switzerland. Calais and Boulogne were to remain in Allied hands, as was Dunkirk, and a Royal Naval Air Service presence was maintained in Dunkirk throughout the war. 'Liberated' Lille ended up on the German side of the line, but at the end of September, Ostend and Antwerp were still to play for.

Churchill took a close personal interest in his aviators based at Dunkirk and visited them regularly. He was on his way to one of these visits on the evening of 3 October when he was recalled to London to a meeting with senior members of the government. They were discussing the news that the Belgians had decided to evacuate Antwerp. No doubt at his own suggestion – he always marched towards the smell of cordite – he was despatched to Antwerp that night to investigate the situation and to try and persuade the Belgians to hold on. Although it controlled the Scheldt River and was a significant port, Antwerp was not critical to the British cause. However, if it had been held, it would have been a major handicap to the German one. So it was always likely that the Germans would be prepared to fight harder for it than the British. Churchill staked the largely unprepared Naval Division, and his reputation, on Antwerp and he lost. He got out in time and although his reputation was badly hit, it survived. About 1,500 men did not get out and were either taken prisoner or interned in the Netherlands, but they too survived. For a further 200 men, there was no survival.

Bad news continued to arrive at the Admiralty in quick succession. On 15 October, the cruiser HMS *Hawke* was torpedoed off the east coast of Scotland with the loss of 500 lives. Twelve days later, the super dreadnought HMS *Audacious* was lost off the coast of Ireland to a mine. Although there was no loss of life, the sinking of this new battleship of 25,000 tons so early in the war was a major shock, especially as in the course of the ten hours that elapsed between the mine strike and her abandonment, there was nothing the crew or any of the several attendant warships could do in the way of damage control to save her. It demonstrated that the new capital ships were not as immune to underwater damage as had been hoped. *Audacious* suffered a large hit in two major compartments without having been properly closed up for action, and inadequate damage control was a factor in her destruction. This loss was sufficiently important for it to be kept a secret, although the use of the liner *Olympic* as part of the rescue flotilla meant that this was a forlorn hope. Within days, her sinking was all over the German and American press. The inquiry into her loss found that significant design and construction flaws were a major factor in her sinking.[1] Not all this was known at the time, but there was a sense of deep unease that a new capital ship should have been lost so easily. There must have been something wrong. She was in fact the only dreadnought battleship to be lost in action in the entire war on either side. Five days after this blow, on 31 October, the newly refitted and only serving seaplane carrier HMS *Hermes* was torpedoed and sunk in the Dover Straits, having delivered much-needed aircraft reinforcements to Dunkirk.

There was no respite from disaster. The following day, 1 November, Rear Admiral Christopher Cradock, perhaps over-reacting to Troubridge's failure to engage the enemy more closely in the Mediterranean, did so too closely in the Pacific off Coronel on the coast of Chile. The cruisers *Good Hope* and *Monmouth* both went down with all hands, all 1,600 of them, including the gallant Cradock himself. This loss was to be avenged the following month by Vice Admiral Doveton Sturdee at the Battle of the Falklands, but it was yet another blow to British prestige, not to mention the loss of so many men, again so early in the war.

On 11 November, another torpedo gunboat, the *Niger*, was torpedoed in the Downs, a stretch of water between the Goodwin Sands and the Kent coast which had been used for centuries as a relatively safe anchorage.

In the midst of this list of troubles, at the end of October, the First Sea Lord, Prince Louis of Battenburg, had been forced to resign. It is widely thought that he was hounded out of office because of his German parentage. However, while being a perfectly competent admiral, he was probably not the man to lead the Navy in a world war. Moreover, he was felt within the Service to be too subservient to the First Lord, Churchill, whose malign interference was blamed for most difficulties. Churchill and Prime Minister Asquith, their political noses sniffing for a scapegoat, let him go with barely a murmur. The fire-eating Jackie Fisher was recalled to the post he had retired from in 1910. Although Churchill no doubt thought that his old friend would be as compliant as Battenberg, he would be proved wrong and, when the new First Sea Lord went the following year, he would take the First Lord with him.

Thus the early success of Heligoland had been supplanted in the minds of the public by an apparently endless litany of losses and failures. Fed on a diet of jingoistic hype, and having paid for the world's most powerful navy, the British public then expected glorious things from it. Notwithstanding the colourful, but ultimately inconsequential, exploits of Samson and his men of the Royal Naval Air Service in Belgium and France, the public were destined to be disappointed. The German High Seas Fleet remained substantially intact throughout the war. British casualties in ships and men outnumbered German casualties two to one. For many of the sailors themselves the war was to become an endless, uncomfortable tedium of North Sea patrols, eventful only for the foulness of the weather, and barely relieved by rest in the hauntingly beautiful but austere, inhospitable anchorage at Scapa Flow. Even when they returned to lick their wounds from gallant and furious action, they were not always appreciated – as the ship's company of HMS *Warspite* discovered when she limped, badly damaged, into Rosyth from Jutland only to be pelted with coal and taunted for 'running away' by workmen on the Forth Bridge.[2] A nation bred on the glories of Trafalgar would be satisfied with nothing less than a repeat performance. Indeed, it has been said that 'the Royal Navy in 1914 was almost totally unprepared for war and remained in that condition for most of the period 1914-1918.'[3]

And yet, and yet ... imperfect instrument of war that it may have been, the Royal Navy proved to be powerful enough, efficient enough and stout-hearted enough to be the ultimate instrument of victory. Its command of the seas allowed the Army's sea lines of communication to the Continent and the rest of the world to function throughout the war without serious challenge. Its tactical and doctrinal shortcomings were thrown into relief by its failure to give Britain the spectacular victory at Jutland that she craved; but Jutland, if not decisive, was a strategic victory nonetheless. The German Imperial High Seas Fleet remained successfully contained in the North Sea and the Baltic, and eventually, after another major attempt, gave up its strategy of trying to ambush detached portions of the Grand Fleet. The U-boat stranglehold, which nearly throttled Britain, was broken just in time. And in maintaining the distant blockade on Germany and her allies, in the words of Basil Liddell Hart, 'it was to do more than any other factor towards winning the war for the Allies.'[4] Even if Liddell Hart was only half right, the taxpaying British public did indeed get their money's worth from their navy. But it did not seem that way at the time. And it certainly did not look that way in the first three months of the First World War.

What was the Navy doing? Surely it should have begun the war by attacking and destroying the German fleet? Instead, in the first three and half months of the war, it had let the *Goeben* and *Breslau* escape, thirteen of its warships had been sunk, including a new capital ship, together with a slew of merchant vessels. And they had lost nearly 4,500 men killed. Nearly 2,000 men of one of the two naval brigades of the Royal Naval Division had also been lost – killed, imprisoned or interned at Antwerp. The fall of Antwerp, because of Churchill's close association with it, was also somehow attributed to the Navy. Instead of fulfilling the hopes and dreams of the population, the Navy had brought little else but bad news and there was not much to show for it. Churchill felt keenly that, with the Army performing gallantly in the public eye in France, his Navy had been unfairly cast in shadow. Little wonder then that he wrote afterwards : 'I do not remember any period when the weight of the War seemed to press more heavily upon me than those months of October and November, 1914.' The resentment and self-justification stands out from the pages of his memoirs. Little wonder also then that Churchill encouraged Sueter to try and repeat the success achieved by destroying a Zeppelin in its shed in Düsseldorf from the air.

But with Antwerp in enemy hands, the question of a mounting base for a similar feat was problematical. None of the bases from which the British were operating was now within range of known Zeppelin sheds. But what about French bases? The French had a balloon base at Belfort, a mere 20 miles from the German border. And a hundred miles across that border was the home of all Zeppelins and the very lair of Count von Zeppelin himself: the great construction sheds at Friedrichshafen on the shores of Lake Constance. Perhaps the French might be prevailed upon to have a go at them? France had led the world in the early days of heavier-than-air aviation and they probably had aircraft with the required range and lift capability. But they had no experience at all in this sort of operation. Furthermore, all was quiet on the Franco-German front in that area and the French were quite happy that it should remain so. They had higher priorites elsewhere. Moreover, dirigibles did not present the critical threat to French assets that they did to the British and the French therefore did not share the pressing urgency to destroy them. If they were to attack from Belfort, would not the Germans retaliate by attacking Belfort where there were virtually no defences at all? So the French, for entirely logical reasons, did not think much of Churchill's idea. Even if it were possible, it was untimely and inconvenient.

However, such considerations did not stand for long in the way of Churchill's will. If it was at all physically possible, he would make it happen. In this instance, Churchill's will happily coincided with a willingness on the part of the French to compromise. Yes, they would agree to let the British mount their own raid from the French base at Belfort '*à condition que* ...' On condition that the utmost secrecy should be observed and that even after the raid had taken place – if indeed it were to take place – the location of the point of departure was to remain a secret. These were conditions that the British would be quite happy to meet. So the raid was on.

The man to whom Sueter turned to plan and organise this raid was a colourful, restless, imaginative character by the name of Noel Pemberton Billing. Pemberton Billing's early years had been spent as a wandering labourer in South Africa. He had seen action as a soldier in the Boer War where he had been slightly wounded twice, and he had been an aide to the Commander-in-Chief, General Sir Redvers Buller.

He was a man who would try anything. He once got a job as a chauffeur before he had even learned to drive, and taught himself on the job. He had turned his hand to the widest variety of other enterprises. He had been an actor on theatrical tours, he had started up a number of ill-thought-out business ventures in South Africa, Brussels and England, and his fortunes had alternated frequently between wealth and penury. He had qualified for the Bar from a standing start in less than two months and had devised a national insurance, old-age pension and national health scheme which predated by many years that which was eventually introduced. He had invented and patented a large number of unlikely and less-than-entirely-useful devices, and he had become fascinated with flight when the Wright brothers arrived in Europe in 1908. He had built himself a glider and launched himself off the roof of his house several times and, in February 1909, he had founded his own aerodrome and workshops for budding aircraft manufacturers at South Fambridge on the River Crouch in Essex. He it was who had learned to fly in twenty-four hours for a £500 wager. He also built his own aircraft. One day long after he sold it, the firm that he started would become Supermarine Aviation Ltd, the company which produced the Spitfire of the Second World War, but he himself was never very successful as an aircraft manufacturer. Neither was he a skilled pilot. When he had insisted on demonstrating his first aircraft himself, he had succeeded only in crashing it and putting himself in hospital for a month.

Broke, depressed and still in pain from his aircraft crash injuries, he was sitting on the beach at Lancing one day, reflecting upon his chequered past and contemplating his bleak future, when his eye lit upon a notice announcing that the foreshore was for sale. Without any money changing hands – it couldn't because he hadn't any – he managed to persuade the vendor to give him a three-month option to purchase. He then threatened to build a casino, a pleasure garden and started building wooden bungalows. Amid the consequent uproar he finally agreed to relinquish his right to purchase for the sum of £2,000. He was rich again.

One of his next ventures was dealing in yachts. He was asked by a fellow yacht dealer to recover a steam yacht which had been bought but not paid for and was now lying alongside at Monaco. Pemberton Billing put a picked crew on one of his own motor yachts, and sailed to Monaco. After studying the movements of the other boat's crew, he chose a moment when their master was playing the tables in the casino. His men invited the 'owner's' crew on board his yacht and spiked their drinks. When this had had the desired effect, the crew were gently carried ashore and laid out on the jetty. He then took over the unpaid-for yacht and set sail, towing it behind his own craft. On the way back to England, he encountered irate consuls in France and official pickets in Gibraltar, all trying to arrest him but, one way or another, he gave them all the slip, shepherded both boats through filthy weather and brought his prize in triumph home to Southampton where he was richly rewarded.

By 1914, Noel Pemberton Billing was a widely known figure in the motor racing, boating and aviation worlds. This free-wheeling maverick, a 'lover of fast aircraft, fast cars, fast boats, and fast women',[5] enjoyed the attention he attracted to himself. His enthusiasm for flying was not matched with success at selling his aircraft. He tried again and again unsuccessfully to get Commodore Murray Sueter in the Admiralty to place orders for his aircraft, but Sueter was not interested. Pemberton Billing's aircraft were never the match of their designer's claims or ambitions. But Sueter had other plans for Pemberton Billing. The latter may not have been held in any great esteem as an aircraft manufacturer, but his daring, resource and courage had been well proved. So it was that to this strange, unscrupulous, buccaneering, reckless, polymath personality Sueter turned to plan and execute the next attempt at destroying the Zeppelin in its lair. It was arranged for him to be granted a temporary commission as a sub lieutenant in the Royal Naval Volunteer Reserves. It was highly unconventional to place such responsibility on the shoulders of such a junior officer, especially as everybody else involved was senior in rank to him. But Noel Pemberton Billing was no ordinary sub lieutenant and never let his lowly rank cramp his style. Born in 1881, thus making him thirty-three years old in 1914, he made up in age and experience what he lacked in rank.

In spite of the dubious, unpredictable side of Pemberton Billing's character, he was well qualified for the task that Sueter had set him. It was just the sort of adventure that he revelled in and he certainly had the imagination, the age and authority – his junior rank notwithstanding – to bring an unconventional approach to the mission and make it work.

The raid itself was to be led by Squadron Commander Philip Shepherd, who was told simply that he would be the leader of an air raid in which four aircraft would take part. Squadron Commander Edward Featherstone Briggs was to be his deputy. Flight Commander John Babington, Flight Lieutenant Sidney Sippe and Flight Sub Lieutenant Roland Cannon, all of the Royal Naval Air Service, were chosen as pilots. Briggs and Sippe had been prominent participants in the armoured car adventures and Sippe had been a test pilot for Avro before the war. Cannon was to be the spare number. None of the officers knew the names of the others nominated, or where they were going, or what they would do when they got there. Security was tight and they were simply told that they would be conducting 'special duties'.

It would have been a relatively straightforward matter to fly the aircraft across the Channel, and then in a couple of hops, to Belfort. The ground crew and stores would have gone by road or train. But it was assumed that Belfort's proximity to the Swiss and German border would mean that anything outwardly unusual or untoward that happened there would be reported to the German authorities. So to ensure complete security, and to meet the conditions placed upon them by the French, other arrangements would have to be made.

The aircraft selected was the Avro 504. This two-seater biplane first came into production in 1913 and had already established its credentials as a graceful, easy-to-handle, dependable aircraft. It had a 36-foot wingspan and, when powered by the Gnome 80hp rotary engine, it flew at 62 mph; it had a ceiling of 13,000 feet. It was well suited for this operation because, as well as having an endurance of some four and a half hours, it was relatively easy to assemble. Soon it would carry a bomb load of four 20lb Hales bombs on a rack under the fuselage but at this stage nothing like this had been contemplated. Its career as a bomber was short lived as it was quickly superseded by more capable machines, but it was to be the staple trainer for British airmen throughout the war. Over 8,000 Avro 504s were eventually built – more than any other British type of the period – and they continued in service around the world for another twenty years.

The 504 was the first of a long line of bombers produced by Avro over the next fifty years. The designer of the fuselage of the 504 was a young man called Roy Chadwick, who went on to design a variety of successful aircraft for Avro, including the Anson, the Manchester, the Lancaster and the Shackleton. He was killed in an air accident in 1947 at which time he was working on what became the Vulcan bomber, which carried Britain's nuclear deterrent. The last Vulcan squadron was disbanded in 1984, by which time Chadwick's handiwork had been seen in operational service in British military aviation for over seventy years.

The Avro 504 was usually a two seater with the seats one behind the other on the fuselage, with head and shoulders protruding into the open air. The observer or trainee sat in the front seat, with the pilot behind. For this operation there was no requirement for a second crewman and fuel would be at a premium. So an extra fuel tank had been fitted in the vacant forward seat, the opening of which was covered over with fabric.

Briggs was told to make arrangements with the aircraft manufacturing firm Messrs A V Roe & Co at their Park Works at Newton Heath in Manchester for the packing of four new aeroplanes, and such spare parts as he thought were necessary, into packing cases. He was instructed to make what arrangements he could for attaching four Hales bombs to each aircraft. He was also told to select the minimum number of riggers necessary to assemble and erect the packed aircraft when uncrated.

Babington was instructed to select six of the best 80hp Gnome rotary engines he could find on his station and the necessary spare parts, and the minimum number of skilled mechanics to install the engines in the aircraft. A ground crew of eleven mechanics and riggers was detailed off.

Cannon, who was a pilot in the Royal Naval Volunteer Reserve and had not been long in the Service, was simply told to stand by and wait for further orders.

They were all told to equip themselves with warm clothes, sleeping bags and blankets. For naval personnel used to living in either ships or bases, this caused some speculation. Did this really mean that they were going somewhere cold? In typical Service fashion they wondered if in fact it was an indication that they would find themselves in the tropics.

Noel Pemberton Billing was given a remarkably free hand by Sueter, which was probably the best way to employ his unusual talents. To begin with, he was the only man who knew what the target of the mission was to be. Pemberton Billing confided in one man, Lieutenant Frank Brock, Royal Navy, of the eponymous firework manufacturers. Brock later played an important part in developing the incendiary ammunition that was eventually to bring Zeppelins down in the air, and was destined to be killed during the amphibious raid on the Belgian port of Zeebrugge in 1918. On this occasion, however, he and Pemberton Billing embarked on another amphibious operation of a very different kind. During the last week of October 1914, only a day or so after Brock's wedding, the pair of them set off to France in Pemberton Billing's conspicuous white racing car in plain clothes. They arrived at Belfort on 24 October and there they made all the arrangements with the French authorities for the eventual arrival and secret accommodation of the aircraft and men who would conduct the raid. The French, having been lukewarm – even indifferent – to the raid at the political level were open handed and unstinting with their assistance at the operational level. One senses that the commander at Belfort and his men deeply deplored that fact that it was not they who were doing the raid, but they afforded every possible help to Pemberton Billing and the British aviators.

Because it was assumed that Germany would have spies watching this balloon base, the British airmen would be confined to the inside of the large hangar throughout their stay before the raid. Having sorted out the administration, Pemberton Billing then turned his attention towards conducting a thorough reconnaissance of the target. Very little was known about the closely guarded Zeppelin complex at Friedrichshafen, so he and Brock set off in the famous white car in civilian clothes to the Swiss border. There they bluffed their way across the frontier pretending to be commercial travellers and motored on to Romanshorn on the southern shore of Lake Constance. The Zeppelin works at Friedrichshafen were directly opposite on the northern shore.

Equipping himself with maps of the area, Pemberton Billing approached some local fishermen who pointed out to him the Zeppelin installations across the lake on the northern shore 7 miles away. He decided that long-range reconnaissance was not sufficient so he persuaded one of the fishermen to take him and Brock across Lake Constance at night in order that he could do a close-in recce. After a night sail across the lake, he was dropped off at a quiet spot near Friedrichshafen and it was agreed that he should be picked up at the same place the following night. Pemberton Billing left Brock with the fisherman to help ensure that he would indeed return for him. He laid up for the rest of the night and in the morning set off on foot to see what he could see.

The Zeppelin installations were in several different places. The floating airship shed by the shore was no longer used for Zeppelins. It was now serving as a hangar for seaplanes which were being manufactured at an aircraft factory a few hundred yards away. Inland from the factory was an airship shed and further inland still, about a kilometre from the lake, was the airship factory, building yard and workshops. This complex was to be the target. There was also a gasometer nearby. Pemberton Billing walked around Friedrichshafen locating these points and noting on his map what he could see of their defences.

Noel Pemberton Billing was a tall, striking figure who usually wore a monocle. It would have been difficult for him to remain inconspicuous at the best of times. Indeed, he probably looked like what many Germans might have thought to be the stereotypical English gentleman. No doubt he tried to be discrete, but he was untrained in the art of covert reconnaissance and discretion was never his strong suit. The Zeppelin works were closely guarded and, unsurprisingly, he soon aroused suspicions. Troops were alerted and he sensed that he had been discovered. He found an empty house near the factory and entered hoping that he could hide therein until the evening. He would then make good his escape and head to the shore for the rendezvous with Brock and the fisherman.

He lay for some hours in the house until the evening shadows gathered and was just about to leave when a large car drove up to the house and stopped outside the front. He watched with horror as three German officers dismounted and walked towards the house, leaving their driver in the car. Pemberton Billing was desperate. No doubt realising that his capture would compromise the whole operation, and not relishing the prospect of spending the rest of the war as a prisoner in Germany, he looked around the room for something he could use as a weapon. Seeing a heavy metal ornamental lion on the mantelpiece, he grabbed it and climbed out of the window, lowering himself to the ground at the back as the German officers entered the front. He then padded round the outside of the house to the car at the front. Approaching it from the rear, he struck the driver on the head with the ornamental lion and knocked him out. Dragging the unconscious man out of his seat and dumping him on the road, he climbed in and drove off followed by a fusillade of shots from the

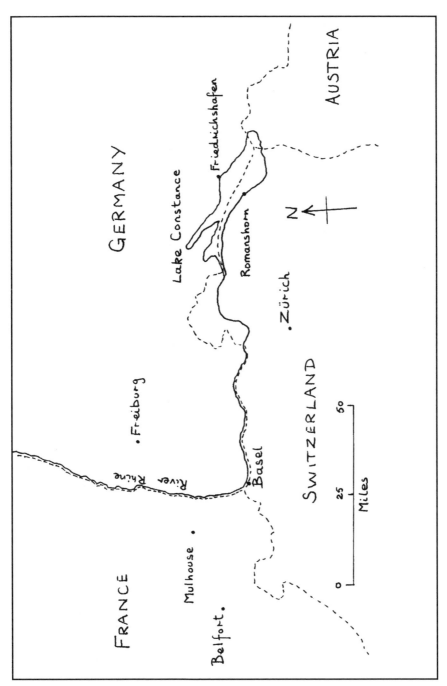

Map 2 - Belfort to Friedrichshafen, November 1914.

German officers. Haring his way through Friedrichshafen at night, he found his direction to the lake shore. Brock and the fisherman had not let him down. They were waiting at the rendezvous and they all made it safely back across Lake Constance to the Swiss side. Pemberton Billing kept the metal lion as a souvenir of his adventure for the rest of his life.

It is not known if the novelist John Buchan ever met Noel Pemberton Billing, or heard of his adventures, but it is just possible that they met in South Africa during the Boer War. Notwithstanding that the only possible original source for this story must have been the man himself, is it conceivable that if Buchan's Richard Hannay was inspired by anyone, it was Pemberton Billing?

Just what information Pemberton Billing gleaned with his hare-brained exploit is not clear, nor if that information was of any use to the pilots who were to conduct the raid. Nor is it clear what conclusions the Germans came to and what they did about it, if anything. But there does not seem to be any evidence that the mission was prejudiced by the German discovery of the spy.

Meanwhile four new untested Avro 504s were duly packed in kit form into large wooden cases. Someone – probably Pemberton Billing – had the bright idea to paint large letters of the Cyrillic alphabet in red on the outside of the cases. Perhaps he was inspired by the rumour current at the time that large numbers of Imperial Russian troops had landed in Scotland and were en route to reinforce the Western Front in France. (They had of course been seen by hundreds of people, and any doubt that they might indeed be Russian was dispelled by the fact that they still had snow on their boots when they arrived in this country.) There was certainly no outward indication of the true contents of the packing cases which were dispatched to Southampton and loaded on board the SS *Manchester Importer*. Briggs, Babington, Cannon and the ground crew were ordered to join her on 10 November. Still none of the party knew what the other members were up to, and only Squadron Commander Shepherd had the vaguest idea of what the purpose of the operation was. He and Sippe would travel separately. Those on the ship were told that final instructions would arrive before the ship sailed. Not even the ship's captain would confirm its destination, although they all assumed it would be France. All awaited the arrival of money and the much promised further instructions.[6]

At the last moment, just before the ship was due to sail and the gangway was about to be hoisted aboard, the instructions arrived in the form of Pemberton Billing driving a white mud-spattered sports car and wearing his own interpretation of a naval officer's uniform. His car swept round the corner of the nearest warehouse, pulled up alongside the foot of the gangway and skidded to a halt. Out stepped our man wearing a strange but immaculate uniform. With glittering gold buttons which somehow seemed to be in the wrong places, a silk shirt and wearing his hat at a Beatty-like rakish angle with a white cover more usually worn in summer, his monocle and a diamond tie pin, he looked as if he had stepped out of Gilbert and Sullivan's *HMS Pinafore*.

Dumfounded by this apparition, the party of pilots was nevertheless much relieved that it had arrived in time. At last they would know something. Pemberton Billing advanced up the gangway carrying in one hand a small sack and in the other a parcel of papers. 'Hello,' he said and with a dazzling smile handed the papers to Briggs, before dropping the little sack with a resounding clunk on the deck. As the ship's siren sounded and the crane started to lift the gangway, he whispered conspiratorially to Briggs, 'See you on the other side,' and scampered back down the gangway to the quay. As the ship drew away, they saw their operatic impresario character in his white sports car whisk off at a speed worthy of Toad of Toad Hall and disappear round the nearest dockyard shed.

The 'other side' could only mean France, but where on the other side were they bound for? This was finally confirmed by the ship's captain once they had sailed. They were bound for Le Havre. They examined the presents brought by Pemberton Billing and wondered how he was going to get to the other side before they did. The bag contained a bundle of French banknotes and 500 gold sovereigns. Briggs, having looked at the papers, now knew the final destination, but the others were still not let in on the secret.

When they arrived at Le Havre the following morning, they were both surprised and relieved to find Pemberton Billing waiting for them, this time in a less sensational naval uniform. He had travelled over on the cross-Channel packet. And not only that, on a truck at the end of a train which was standing almost alongside the berth there was the white racing car. It transpired that this was 'their' train which Pemberton Billing had arranged with the French authorities. They proceeded to transfer the packing cases with their Russian markings. During this evolution, the electric power plant broke down so they had finally to load them, heaving and sweating, in their shirtsleeves. Soon the train, with its white sports car and conspicuous huge packing cases with their red Russian markings, was trundling across France, skirting round Paris and beyond. There was one stop at some quiet place on the journey. Here the white car was unloaded and it disappeared with Pemberton Billing, now in plain clothes, waving and saying, 'See you at the other end.' The 'other end' was the railway siding near the airship hangar near Belfort, where indeed their man was waiting.

Unwilling to expose his Russian marked crates to the scrutiny of the locals, he directed that they wait until dark in a disused siding before they were unloaded, and then once more the crates were manhandled off the train and the great doors of the hangar, which had opened just sufficiently to swallow up the pilots, the ground crew and their strange-looking luggage, rolled together again. The pilots felt like prisoners in a vast, cold, draughty, iron and concrete cavern. There was no sign of Shepherd or Sippe.

The men were told that on no account were they to leave the hangar. Pemberton Billing would be their link to the outside world. They would eat, sleep and work until the last moment, out of sight of prying eyes. By now they had guessed that they were going to attack Friedrichshafen. Pemberton Billing produced his maps, told them of his plans for the raid and gave them such information as he had gathered. The pilots did not feel this amounted to anything very much; there were no photographs or sketches. But they felt that there could surely be no mistake about recognising an airship hangar close to the end of a large lake. Except in the case of a thick fog, one could hardly fail to find it. They did not take much interest in what might be described as the tactical aspects of the forthcoming operation – the business of getting there overshadowed all other considerations.

None of the pilots had ever dropped a bomb before. It occurred to them therefore that the secrecy might have been overdone, and that it might have been a good idea to have done some bombing practice before leaving Britain.

They lost no time in unpacking the aircraft and engine crates. Forty-eight hours later, on 14 November, four Avro 504s were assembled complete inside the hangar and the engines had been run and tested. The bomb attachments – primitive though they were – gave a little trouble, but that was easily overcome. The bombs themselves were suspended under the fuselage, two on either side. To release them, the pilot merely had to pull at a series of four wires which, in turn, pulled out the split pins which held the bombs in place. They had bomb sights of a sort. Experimental work had been done before the war on bomb sights and a basic sight comprising a board with two nails in it, and a spirit level, had been tried. The board was held level and the two nails, when they were lined up with the target, indicated the moment for release. This fixed device would indicate the correct dropping angle only for one specific altitude and ground speed. In addition, the mechanics had fixed up a series of sighting pins on the outside of the fuselage of the machines, but it nearly broke the pilots' necks when they put their heads over the side to use these. Besides, the sighting angles didn't really correspond to anything that they could see, so they had no intention of using these primitive bomb sights.

Later in the war, a more complex device was created whereby the nails, or the sight, were adjusted according to a set of tables for height and ground speed.[7] This seemed sensible enough in theory but, for the pilot, it was no simple matter. He had to know his altitude, estimate his ground speed, consult the tables and set his sight accordingly. He then had to fly straight and level towards the target maintaining the correct altitude and ground speed, holding on to the sight while looking through it until the nails lined up, and then release his bombs at the correct moment. And all this without taking into account anything the enemy might be doing to take his eye off the ball. Work continued well into the war to try and produce an effective user-friendly sight, especially in the Royal Naval Air Service. But it remained an imperfectly solved problem right through to the war's end when still 'leaders simply judged when to release their bombs' and the remainder followed suit.[8]

These pilots were not about to inflict upon themselves the additional cross of an uncertain bomb sight. Anyhow, there was no time for that sort of thing now. They would manage alright. They would simply rely upon their own eyeballs.

These particular aircraft had no radios – the weight and size of early receivers and transmitters were significant drawbacks, as was the question of power generation. Also, the noise of the wind and the engine conspired to make it very difficult to hear signals, and microphones too were in their infancy. Transmission was by tapping out Morse code, which required pilots to be expert signallers. The first successful airborne tests, in which Samson had been a leading light, had taken place in 1912, with power being generated with a bicycle chain linked to the engine's crankshaft. The impetus to carry radios when operating over the sea was strong. If one came down on the sea and survived, one would still be entirely at the mercy of the elements unless one had been able to transmit news of one's plight. Indeed, on one occasion, the aircraft engine had failed and the aircrew had landed safely at sea. They were found and rescued because of their radio transmissions.

John Babington had been involved in these radio trials in May 1913. While flying along the coast between the Isle of Grain and North Foreland, he remained in touch with ground stations throughout the flight and sent his felicitations to the Royal Yacht which was taking the King on a visit to Germany. By November 1914, communications had been developed to the point where ranges of over 130 miles had been achieved. But radios were still heavy and the priorities on this mission were bombs and fuel, and besides, what would be the point of a radio? Who would the pilots talk to and what would they tell them? They were either going to make it, in which case people would find out when they got home, or they weren't; and people would find that out too when they didn't get home.

Shepherd and Sippe finally arrived by car from Dijon on the morning of 15 November after struggling their way through a seemingly interminable series of French sentry posts on the way. The weather was suitable for an attempt but the two new arrivals were exhausted after their travels so it was decided to wait until the following day. The next day weather was bad and it had turned bitterly cold as the temperature went down to minus 7° Celsius. The pilots felt that the floor of the hangar upon which they slept, ate and played cards couldn't have been harder or colder, whatever happened. Babington wondered if a bed of nails might not have been more comfortable to sleep on than the concrete floor of a French dirigible balloon hangar in winter. It would certainly have been warmer.

However, the pilots did find a moment to examine the ground from which they were going to take off. Belfort was a balloon station and the aerodrome had not been prepared for heavier-than-air craft. The ground was hard, but rough and stony, so was far from ideal. They selected a portion for use as a take-off runway and with the help of the French balloon station staff, they removed a length of wire fencing and some of the larger and looser stones. They were concerned that, with the extra fuel and the bombs, they would be carrying just about as much of an overload as their 80hp engines could be expected to lift off the ground. There was more than a chance that on the rough surface, the wheels and undercarriage would buckle while taking off – even without an overload. As they only had a limited supply of undercarriage wheels and spare parts they therefore decided it was better not to risk making any preliminary test flights, which meant that they would launch the operation with untested machines. If, when airborne, the machines proved, for instance, to be nose heavy, or flying 'one wing down', the pilots could compensate with elastic bungees on the control sticks – an early form of automatic pilot. Right or wrong, this 'no test' decision fitted in with the security precautions and ensured that no shortage of spare parts would prevent them starting.

Preparations were now complete, but their French hosts had one last surprise to throw at them. They demanded that whatever they were to carry in the way of maps and papers, there should be nothing in or on the machines which would give the enemy any indication of where they had come from. Should they be shot down in Germany, there should be nothing which might give away the fact that they had launched from a French base. Given the range of the aircraft, it is difficult to imagine the Germans thinking that they might have come from anywhere other than France. Where else could they possibly have come from? Nevertheless, the French were quite insistent on this point. They wanted to disown any involvement in the raid whatsoever, which meant that the pilots would not be allowed to carry any maps of any part of France. This might not matter a great deal

Captain Murray Sueter, Director of the Admiralty Air Department and key driver of progress in early naval aviation. (*FAA Museum*)

Wing Commander Charles Samson, one of the first four Royal Navy pilots and dynamic innovator and pioneer of naval aviation. (*FAA Museum*)

Winston Churchill, First Lord of the Admiralty and budding pilot. (*Historic Images*)

Charles Samson at the controls of a Short 27 at Eastchurch 1911. (*FAA Museum*)

SHORT 100 h.p. (Gnome) Seaplane - improved type - off Gravesend.
Pilot :- Commander Samson.   Passenger :- Rt Hon. Winston Churchill (First Lord of Admlty)

Charles Samson taking Winston Churchill up in a Short seaplane in 1914. (*FAA Museum*)

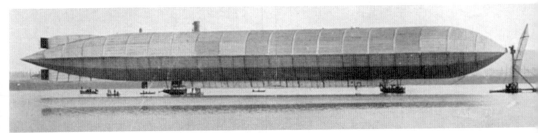

Britain's 'Zeppelin', the *Mayfly*, which never flew. (*Historic Images*)

The end of the *Mayfly*. (*National Archive*)

HMS *Hermes*, the first aircraft carrier, sinking after being torpedoed in the Channel in August 1914.
(*FAA Museum*)

The ROYAL FLYING CORPS contingent of the 1914 BRITISH EXPEDITIONARY FORCE consisting of No's 2, 3, 4, and 5, Squadrons flew from this field to AMIENS between 13 and 15 August 1914.

The field above Dover from where the first air force deployed to war. (*David Storrie*)

RNAS armoured car with revolving turret of 1914, and forerunner of the tank. (*Historic Images*)

The first strategic bomber: a Sopwith three-seater tractor biplane with Reggie Marix at the controls. (*FAA Museum*)

The Sopwith Tabloid: early strategic bomber flown by Reggie Marix and Spenser Gray attacking Düsseldorf and Cologne, and with a speed of 92 mph was the fastest aircraft of its day. (*Historic Images*)

Major Eugene Gerrard Royal Marine Light Infantry, one of the first four Royal Navy pilots. He accompanied Charles Collet on the first raid on Düsseldorf. (*FAA Museum*)

Eugene Gerrard at the controls of a Farman F20. (*Historic Images*)

Lieutenant Charles Collet, Royal Marine Artillery, the first strategic bomber pilot. (*Historic Images*)

quadron Commander Spenser Grey: pleaded
with Churchill through the lavatory door for
permission to launch the Düsseldorf/Cologne
aid, and bombed Cologne railway station.
(Illustrated War News)

Flight Lieutenant Reggie Marix, destroyer of the
Zeppelin at Düsseldorf. (*FAA Museum*)

An artist's impression of how the Düsseldorf shed might have contained a second airship next to
the original on the left. Based on nothing more than this drawing on the photograph, the press
speculated that Marix might have destroyed more than one Zeppelin. (Illustrated War News)

Squadron Commander Edward Briggs, led and was shot down on the Friedrichshafen raid. (*Historic Images*)

Flight Lieutenant Sidney Sippe, flew on the Friedrichshafen raid and conducted the first low-level strike in history. (*Historic Images*)

Flight Lieutenant John Babington (later Tremayne), pilot on the Friedrichshafen raid. (*FAA Museum*)

Three newly assembled Avro 504s, ready for the Friedrichshafen raid. These aircraft had never been flown before. From the left, the pilots were Babington, Sippe and Briggs. The fourth, piloted by Roland Cannon, broke its tail skid and did not take off. (*FAA Museum*)

With the ground crew holding the plane back until the last moment, John Babington gets a final briefing before the Friedrichshafen raid. Note the bombs under the fuselage and the rotary engine spewing fumes and castor-oil vapour. (*FAA Museum*)

Edward Briggs's Avro 504 after being shot down during the raid at Friedrichshafen, near the sheds he was trying to destroy. (*FAA Museum*)

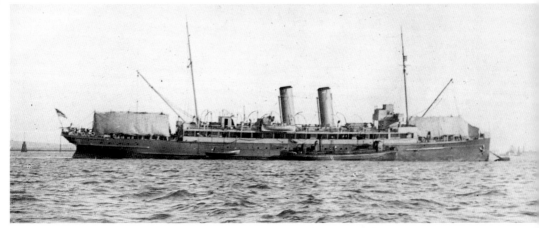

HMS *Riviera*, seaplane carrier on the Cuxhaven raid. Note her canvas hangars. (*FAA Museum*)

Front row from the left: Robert Ross, Douglas Oliver, Arnold Miley and A.B. Gaskell, all pilots on the Cuxhaven raid, although Gaskell's plane did not take off. At centre rear, Cecil Malone, captain of the *Engadine* where the photograph was taken, tactical commander of the air component, and subsequently Britain's first Communist MP. It is thought that Erskine Childers, the spy thriller author who flew as an observer on the Cuxhaven raid, is on his right. (*FAA Museum*)

Captain Cecil Kilner Royal Marine Light Infantry. Childers was his observer on the Cuxhaven raid. (*Historic Images*)

Short Type 74. Seaplanes of this type were flown by Edmonds, Blackburn and Oliver on the Cuxhaven raid. The engine of the fourth, piloted by Bone, would not start. (*Historic Images*)

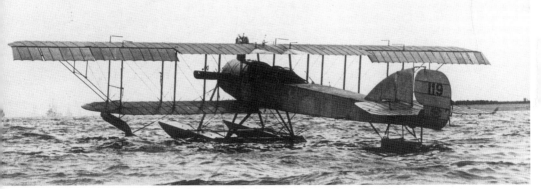

Short Type 81 or 'Folder'. Seaplanes of this type were flown by Ross and Miley on the Cuxhaven raid. A third, piloted by Gaskell, did not take off. (*FAA Museum*)

The Short Type 81 seaplane flown by Robert Ross on the Cuxhaven raid. (*FAA Museum*)

Short Type 135 seaplane flown by Francis Hewlett on the Cuxhaven raid, demonstrating its 'folder' capability. (*Historic Images*)

HM Submarine *E11*, commanded by Lieutenant Commander Martin Nasmith, which rescued five aviators on the Cuxhaven raid. (*FAA Museum*)

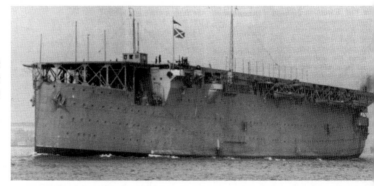

HMS *Argus*, the first through-deck aircraft carrier. (*Historic Images*)

, the first German naval Zeppelin. Commissioned in 1912, destroyed in a storm in 1913 with the loss fourteen out of twenty crew. (*Archive of the Luftschiffbau Zeppelin GmbH*)

The Zeppelin's cargo. Bombs ranging from 22lb to 660lb, together with incendiaries left and right, and a parachute flare in front of the 660 pounder. Bomb loads went from half a ton in 1915 to 4 tons a year later. (*Friedrich Moch*)

3. With 2,000,000 cubic feet of hydrogen, and capable of climbing to over 20,000 feet, she was shot own with the loss of all twenty-four crew in 1917. Note dark underside to counter searchlights, and achine-gun post on top. (*Archive of the Luftschiffbau Zeppelin GmbH*)

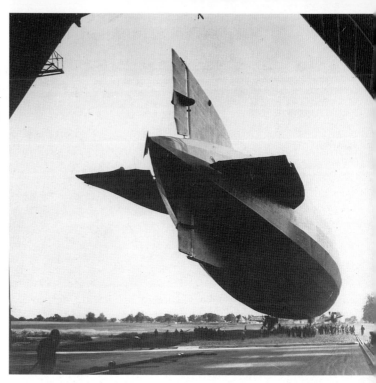

L53 at Friedrichshafen: 'the size of a battleship or an ocean liner'. (*Archive of the Luftschiffbau Zeppelin GmbH*)

The sub-cloud car which crashed to earth near Colchester in 1916, now suspended from the ceiling in the Imperial War Museum, London. The one-man crew climbed in through the sliding hatch on top. It was the smokers who volunteered to man it. (*Catriona Gardiner*)

Korvettenkapitän Peter Strasser, commander of the German Naval Airship Division. A brilliant leader but grossly over-optimistic. (*Archive of the Luftschiffbau Zeppelin GmbH*)

Winston Churchill with Clementine who stopped him qualifying for the pilot's wings, which he wore nevertheless. (*Historic Images*)

Brigadier General David Henderson, the true 'Father of the Royal Air Force'. (*Historic Images*)

Hugh Trenchard, passed-over major of Royal Scots Fusiliers and Marshal of the Royal Air Force, and its most stalwart champion. (*Historic Images*)

Frederick Sykes, erstwhile cavalry trooper, temporary Royal Marine colonel and Chief of the Air Staff. The most able of the early air commanders, but neither Henderson nor Trenchard could work with him. (*Historic Images*)

The German aircraft carrier *Graf Zeppelin* about to be launched in 1938. Neither she nor her sister ship the *Peter Strasser* was completed. (*Historic Images*)

on the outward journey – the German border was only 20 miles away and, once they had spotted Lake Constance, which was impossible to miss, they would be able to orientate themselves easily. But on the return journey it might be decidedly awkward, if for instance the visibility was poor. And so it was to prove.

The weather got colder, wetter and worse. An east wind set in. The hangar could hardly get any colder or more uncomfortable and the pilots got tired of waiting. After a week, the rain and the east wind died down and it became fairly clear to westward. But over Germany to the east, the cloud blanket still held. However, with a west wind, perhaps this would soon clear.

By now life on the floor of a hangar in winter was beginning to have its effect on the pilots, and in particular, upon the health of Squadron Commander Philip Shepherd. Unable to sleep or keep his food down, it looked increasingly as if he would be unable to fly. However, some spirit moved him into deciding after all to test his machine in a trial flight. The others stood fast on their previous decision to trust on luck, elastic bungees and the skill of their riggers. Shepherd's plane never got off the ground. Even though his tanks were not full and he had no bombs on board, he failed to negotiate a piece of rough ground. One of his wheels collapsed, the undercarriage was buckled, the propeller smashed and the wing tip skid broken. His aircraft was removed back to the hangar where it was repaired.

Notwithstanding the security implications, Shepherd was shipped off to a hotel in Belfort and Edward Briggs took over command of the pilots. Roland Cannon took over Shepherd's repaired aircraft. The pilots now persuaded Pemberton Billing that if they were forced to live in the hangar much longer, their health would go the same way as Shepherd's, and then there would be no operation at all. So they all moved into the hotel and a car was arranged to ferry them to and from the hangar.

On 21 November, the wind at last swung round to the west. It was cold and started to clear overhead. They watched the clouds being blown back over Germany. In a few hours, the skies over Lake Constance should be clearing too. They had waited so long for this moment. They now waited as long as they dared. If they started too soon, the cloud might not have cleared over Friedrichshafen. If they left it too late, they might never get back. Without maps of France, and in failing light, they might easily miss France and land up in Switzerland. And if they did get lost, and hadn't run out of fuel, would their second-hand engines last long enough for them to re-orientate themselves and find their way back again?

They quickly dismissed all these doubts from their minds. If they had judged it right, conditions for this time of year were ideal. With winter deepening fast, they could not expect to get a second chance in the foreseeable future. Besides, the prospect of extending this twilight life in the Belfort hangar and the local hotel was a wonderful disincentive for prevarication. At 0930 hrs they rolled open the hangar doors and wheeled out their machines.

They had already worked out their route to the target. It could not be a direct easterly flight because that would infringe Swiss neutrality. They would head 10 degrees north of east for 85 miles, keeping to the north of the River Rhine once they had crossed it beyond Mulhausen, and then 8 degrees south of east for the remaining 38 miles to the target. This would entail flying over the Black Forest Mountains which ascend to 3,500 feet. The direct route would be 123 miles; this route was 126 miles. And this would be the maiden flight for all four aircraft. None of them had been flown before.

All four pilots sat in their seats with their ground crews clustered anxiously around their machines. The riggers and mechanics knew how much depended upon their skill and dedication. There would be no second chance to make adjustments, or to correct mistakes. Everything would have to work first time. Would the engines start? There was quite an art, not to say technique, about the starting process. It had to be done by hand – that is, the propeller had to be swung round by hand, and it had to be properly timed. First the propeller had to be given a preliminary turn or two with the ignition switched off. This was to draw the right mixture and the right quantity of fuel, oil and air into the cylinders – not too much, otherwise there was the risk of the engine bursting into flames. That done, the pilot switched on the ignition. The engine mechanic had to grasp the blade with all his strength and weight, and give it a final swing. That should start the engine. But it didn't always work and in cold weather it was even more uncertain.

'Contact!' The first of four motors spluttered into life and to their immense relief, the other three followed in turn. The pilots had lined up their four machines behind each other so as to give themselves as long a run as possible. There was no question of taking off in formation – there wasn't enough flat ground for that. They faced into a light steady breeze. To make the most of the limited makeshift runway, they planned to make a series of quick-release starts. This involved each aircraft being restrained by the ground crews until the motors were running at full speed, and then being released. One after the other they were let go by the men on the ground and they trundled forward, three minutes apart, gathering speed as they rumbled over the rough ground. Briggs was first at 0945 hrs, then Babington, then Sippe, followed by Cannon flying Shepherd's repaired plane. Briggs, Babington and Sippe lifted clear successfully. As with Shepherd, Cannon's machine once again failed to rise. A second attempt was made. No luck – it just wouldn't lift. In turning round to have third go, his tail skid broke off and his tail was slightly damaged. Any further attempt to move without repair would wreck his tail, so his aircraft was immobilised. Meanwhile the others had taken off and were on their way, disappearing out of sight. With much frustration, Cannon was forced to abort and watch his comrades slowly gain height and disappear. So now there were three.

Once the aircraft were out of sight, Pemberton Billing apparently took himself off in his white racing car across the border to Switzerland to a small hotel 'to await a telephone call with information about the raid from a contact he had made near Friedrichshafen'.[9] It seems unlikely that this was a German national. It is probable that it was a Swiss engineer whose report on the results was recorded later. Or perhaps it was one of his fishermen acquaintances.

So far as the pilots were concerned, they had overcome the first major obstacle. Their bomb armourer, when removing the pins from the fuses, had helpfully pointed out that they had better not try and land anywhere with the bombs still in place – if the undercarriage were to collapse and the aircraft were to sit down on the bombs under the fuselage, they were almost certain to go off. The pilots had no intention of bringing the bombs back with them, or sitting down on them anywhere. But they certainly had their doubts as to whether they could get off the ground without suffering the same fate as Shepherd on his trial flight. However, although Cannon suffered a related fate with his tail skid, three of them were now airborne.

What was more, the rigging of all three aircraft was fine. The aircraft were decidedly nose heavy but they had foreseen that possibility and were able to adjust their rubber bungees to relieve their arms of constant strain. Flying in formation would have been difficult because they had no means of adjusting the speed of the engine. It would have been a coincidence if they had all flown at exactly the same speed. However, they started off with the idea that they might keep in touch with each other. Each took a wide circuit of the airfield, gaining height, and set off more or less together towards the objective. But in reality it was every man for himself.

They took a last look down at the aerodrome and saw their little band of mechanics and riggers waving farewell. Everything had depended upon them. They had worked so hard and with infinite care to see that all should go well. The first fruit, and the test of their labours, lay in the take-off. They had triumphed. They had got three out of four planes into the air. They must be grinning from ear to ear. Now it was up to the pilots.

After gaining a bit of height – a slow business – they headed east. The weather was magnificent. There were a few clouds away in the distance over Germany, but nothing to worry about, and maximum visibility nearly all round the rest of the horizon. The snow shone and glittered on the Alpine peaks and it was bitterly cold. The cover over the vacant front cockpit did nothing to reduce the draught in the pilot's seat. A little hinged windscreen on the front edge of the pilot's cockpit served to break the force of the wind in their faces, and at the same time to intercept some of the castor oil which blew back in the exhaust gases from the engine.

By the war's end bomber aircraft routinely flew at 15,000 feet, and pilots had electrically heated clothing and oxygen supplies. By 1918, they also used whale oil to prevent frostbite. But in 1914, there was no specialised flying clothing. Each pilot wore what he himself chose to provide. Short-length thick overcoats, long woollen scarves, fur or wool-lined flying helmets and thick underclothes were the norm. There were no special boots or shoes. These men had been conscious that they were going to make a very long flight in cold weather and that they could conceivably suffer from frostbite. They had debated what the best precaution might be and it was finally agreed that a little brandy inside the boots and on the socks might be a good idea. Brandy after all gives you a warm feeling inside if you drink it, doesn't it? However, this charmingly naval notion of insulation against the cold had nothing whatsoever to commend itself. Meanwhile, the thrill of actually being on their way was protection enough against the chill.

By the time they reached the Rhine, the planes were still within sight of each other and at about 3,500 feet. As they crossed the Rhine and entered mapped country, the pilots made mental notes of the crossing points and jotted down the reciprocal bearing from their somewhat wavering compasses. If on the return journey they could find their way to the same spot on the Rhine, this reverse course should take them straight back to Belfort. Sippe soon overtook Babington and both he and Briggs slowly drew ahead. Babington found his machine very nose heavy but with difficulty he managed to get it up to over 4,000 feet. Although his engine was running regularly enough, he couldn't get any more power out of it, so he gave up trying to get any higher. Besides, the level of oil in the glass 'pulsator' gauge had fallen and he was concerned that the castor oil in the engine might be too cold already. He feared that ice might form at the exposed forward end of the hollow crankshaft through which petrol, oil and air reached the crank case and the cylinders through spring-loaded valves in the piston heads. This was a risk with these engines. The only thing to do was to keep going and hope he was not too late. The leading pair reached 5,000 feet, passed to the north of Basle and cleared the Black Forest Mountains. Babington also cleared the mountains but skirted some way south of the highest peaks. The following wind increased as they got higher and Babington soon lost sight of Briggs and Sippe. The weather was perfect. The sun shone brilliantly and the few clouds that there were were too high to make any difference. It would surely be impossible to miss the Zeppelin hangars which should be in sight before too long.

Briggs was the first to arrive over the target. He succeeded in dropping all his bombs but came under heavy fire from both machine guns and rifle fire. Sippe reported that he saw shrapnel shells exploding in the area. Briggs probably only completed one pass before his engine failed, either because his fuel tank was badly holed or the fuel line was severed by a bullet. With no engine, he was forced to land as best he could. He somehow managed to get down safely in close proximity to the hangar he had been trying to destroy. Very quickly a number of civilian workmen started to approach his aircraft, quite plainly and unsurprisingly with less than friendly intentions. He drew his pistol, which according to at least one report was empty, and managed to hold them off until a German officer arrived and persuaded him to surrender. Thereafter, in the hands of the German military authorities, he was treated with complete respect and humanity. Briggs was slightly wounded in the head, but it is not certain whether this was sustained in the air or on the ground. The Germans even went so far as to communicate the non-life-threatening nature of his wounds to the British through the American embassy in Berlin.

Thus Edward Briggs, who had been responsible for procuring the aircraft from Avro's, for fixing up the bomb racks – it was he who had thought of fixing elastic bungees to the control sticks and many other things which had solved so many of their day-to day difficulties – and who had taken the burden of leadership when Shepherd had become ill, was now a prisoner of war. So now there were two.

Sydney Sippe didn't see Briggs come down but lost sight of him suddenly when he was over the target. He guessed that Briggs had stirred up a hornets' nest so he decided upon a different approach. Having been a test pilot for Avro's he was almost certainly more experienced and confident than the others. As he arrived at the western end of Lake Constance, he came right down to within 10 feet of the water and continued at this height until he passed the town of Constance to his south. He then turned north skimming across the surface of the lake until he arrived on the northern side. So among the firsts to be claimed by this raid, Sippe could claim to have made the first low-level strike in history.

Thereafter he hugged the northern coast for the remaining 5 miles to the sheds, whereupon he climbed to 1,200 feet. He then dived on the sheds and dropped one bomb in an enclosure in the hope of putting the gunners off their aim and another two bombs into the works and the shed. He noticed up to 500 men in a line by the shed, very probably those same men who were advancing upon Briggs. His fourth bomb failed to release.

Throughout this time he was under heavy fire from the ground. He flew north out of range of the guns and back again over the shed trying to release his bomb, which failed to oblige. He then headed for the waterside still under fire. Near the lake he had another attempt at dislodging his recalcitrant bomb on the aircraft factory at the waterside without success.[10] Coming down to surface level he made good his escape westwards along the lake and somehow found his way back to Belfort without a map of France, but was now faced with the prospect of landing with a 'hung-up' bomb under his fuselage.

The Hales bomb was designed not to arm until the rotating vane on the tail had completed the requisite number revolutions in order to activate the fuse. In theory therefore, it would be safe even if it fell off on landing. But the safety pin had been pulled on this bomb and technological fail-safe mechanisms have an unpleasant habit of not living up to their expectations. There were later incidents in which pilots were blown to bits by their own bombs when they landed under similar circumstances. Sippe of course did not know this, but he surely was aware of the awful possibilities. In later wars, pilots had the option of abandoning their potentially lethal aircraft and descending by parachute. Sippe had no such choice. But he got down safely at Belfort shortly before two o'clock, in spite of one of his wheels crumpling on landing.

The pilots had had strict instructions not to cross the international boundary into neutral Switzerland, even though there was as yet no international agreement that recognised exclusive sovereignty over the air space above national territory. Since the line passed down the centre of the lake, it seems likely that Sippe had indeed breached this instruction on the outward journey, and possibly on the homeward journey as well. The Swiss certainly thought he had and registered a complaint. In their response, the Foreign Office reminded the Swiss of the current state of the law, denied that Sippe had crossed the line, but said that even if he had, it had been a mistake.

John Babington had long since lost sight of his fellow flyers and wondered what he would find when he got to Friedrichshafen. Would the hangars be ablaze? He did a last quick check-up. The toggles on the ends of the four wires that he had to pull to release the bombs were fine. They were arranged so that one could not pull them all at once. But he lined them up so that he could pull them one after the other with the minimum of delay, removing his right-hand glove so that he could feel them better. He had not brought his clumsy Service revolver, but instead he had his cherished German Mauser pistol tethered by a loose lanyard and lying snugly in a bracket ready to use. It was already loaded with a clip of cartridges. He eased off the safety catch. The engine was running smoothly. Nothing more to worry about inside the machine. He was all set.

Everything looked incredibly peaceful, so quiet in the bright sunshine. Out over Lake Constance on the German side of the international boundary, he could already see where Friedrichshafen must be. A ground haze prevented him seeing the details. The approach seemed incredibly slow – and indeed it was. He was at best flying at about 60 mph. He wondered where the other two machines were. Perhaps they were getting into position right ahead and high up above or behind one of those white detached clouds which were hanging about over the head of the lake. They were small clouds like bits of cotton wool – like clouds in Chinese pictures. Onwards his aircraft droned. He knew exactly what he was going to do. He had gone over it in his mind a thousand times.

It would be no good trying to dodge in unseen behind the scattered clouds as they were too high and he couldn't climb up to them. And the German gunners would be on the alert anyhow, for his two companions would be there at any moment if they weren't there already. The sun would be his ally. He would continue straight on until he was in a direct straight line between the sun and the great hangar below. Then he would turn sharp left and dive for the hangar with the sun directly behind him. He knew from what information Pemberton Billing had picked up roughly where the anti-aircraft defences were supposed to be. With luck they would be firing into the sun, if and when they opened fire at him.

But perfect peace seemed to be reigning everywhere. There were still a few minutes to go before the time came for him to turn. He searched the clouds above and ahead for any sign of the other two machines – there was nothing to be seen. Down below, ahead and slightly to the left, where the hangar must be, nothing seemed to be stirring either: no flashes, no flames, no clouds of smoke. But he was still some way off. Was it possible that somewhere along the route the other two machines had come down? Surely it wasn't likely that they had both had engine failures? Aircraft engines were not the most reliable pieces of machinery, but he had chosen the best engines he could find, and their matchless mechanics had lavished care and attention on them. It couldn't be that two out of three engines had failed. Where were they?

He had another quick look at the cloud clusters ahead. Much to his surprise, there was now a group of small, very small, round white blobs in the sky. He had never seen anything like it. And then suddenly he knew what it was. The guns of Friedrichshafen had opened fire. One or the other or both of his companions were going in to the attack.

Whatever else happened or was going to happen, they had made it! He longed to be able to shout this to the waiting group of mechanics and riggers back at Belfort. It was really all their doing. But there was no time for further reflection along these lines. Besides, he hadn't got there yet. He still had plenty of time – too much time it seemed – before he was between the sun and the target, and it would be time for him to turn and begin his attack. Meanwhile, the pattern of shell bursts spread over the skies ahead. He still could not see either of the other two machines so he made a quick note on his writing pad of the time at which the guns had begun to fire.

He was in a fever of excitement. Every second seemed like a long and endless minute. He wiped his goggles which were faintly blurred with engine oil from the exhaust. There are times when, even if somebody else would have been of no real use, it is a sort of relief to have someone there, if only for the purpose of occasionally saying something quite unnecessary to him – or alternatively maintaining an impressive silence. But there was nobody there either to impress silently, or to say anything unnecessary to. He found himself thinking in terms as if he were talking to himself.

The shell bursts were getting closer, or perhaps he was getting closer to them. They were bursting high above his level. How desperately slow the approach was. He was tempted to speed up by sacrificing height but he knew he needed what height he had. He must just keep going.

Suddenly, slightly to the right of him, he saw one of the other machines away down below, as it went past with shrapnel bursting in its rear, heading westwards down the lake at low level, on its way back to France. Which of his companions was it? But there was no time to bother about that. Babington was alright anyhow. A thousand thoughts and questions crowded in upon his mind. Was he too late? Where was the other machine? Had the great hangar been hit? He could make out its shape now, still a bit blurred. Was there a haze around it? Could it be smoke? He couldn't see the other plane. He dismissed his doubts, convincing himself that whatever had happened, there was no reason for him to change his plans. He desperately wanted to increase speed, to hasten the moment when he could turn left and dive on the target. But he mustn't turn too soon! He found himself saying quite slowly and clearly, as if he were speaking to somebody else, 'Keep going, you bloody fool.'

As Babington passed the waterside hangar, he noticed that the door was open and the building empty. He could see the main hangar more clearly now. It was not alight in a mass of sprouting flames. Never mind. At least it meant he was not too late to do anything, and it relieved him of that rather mean anxiety. It was now his turn to have a crack at it. There had been a lull in the firing. But now the guns had opened up again. It was almost time to turn. Although the shell bursts were all still well above him, it was beginning to get noisy. But now at last the Zeppelin sheds below were broad on his left, and above, the sun broad on his right. At last! And what was more, the target seemed to be at just about the right distance away to his left. When he swung round through 90 degrees and thrust the nose of the machine down so that it pointed at the great hangar below, he did not want the angle of descent to be too steep, nor yet to be too flat. If he got too near a vertical dive, the bombs might foul on the undercarriage. He wanted to have just a little time to get the machine travelling like an arrow – straight and steady on the mark – before he let the first bomb go. It might have given him a fraction more time to release the bombs one after the other if he had cut the engine. But he decided not to do that. It might not start again. He'd let it rip. It should stand it alright.

He now banked hard and swung round to the left. Friedrichshafen disappeared under the nose of the machine. He straightened up, thrust the stick forward and forced the nose of the machine down below the far horizon; down until it pointed at the fields in the middle distance; down until it pointed straight at the centre of the great black – or was it grey green? – hangar below. He pushed the hinged windscreen down. It was no use now. The engine was clattering wildly round, but the vibration was not too bad. The air seemed filled with a jumble of sounds. He could see the flash of the guns below. But there was no time to think. The angle of dive was less steep than he had intended. If he let go now, he was afraid that the bombs would fall short, but he still had more than enough height in hand. He eased up a bit.

Before he finally thrust the nose down again, he just had time to see what he had not noticed before: a big shed close alongside the great hangar itself, and on the lakeward side, a large, roughly circular clearing in the middle of which there was an aeroplane with a few scattered figures near to it. It must have been a German machine about to take off. Pemberton Billing had said nothing much about German aircraft at Friedrichshafen. Perhaps he had said there 'might' be some. But they hadn't paid any attention to that. It didn't matter anyhow. It was on the ground and it couldn't do him any harm.

Nose down again – there seemed to be a hell of a racket going on – but he was dead on target. The hangar looked bigger than ever – he had no eyes for anything else. He shouted at himself 'Stand by', a split second later pulled the toggle which released his first bomb at about 950 feet, and groped for the next toggle. 'Don't rush it,' he said to himself, and pulled the next toggle. Two more to go. Yes, there was just time. But why the hell hadn't the hangar burst into flames? Where had the first bomb fallen? Why hadn't it gone off? Or hadn't it had time? Or worse, had the bombs got stuck in their racks? No – surely not.

He wrenched at the next toggle at 450 feet with his plane nearly vertical. The German gunners had difficulty in adjusting their fire as he rapidly changed altitude and shrapnel kept bursting above and beyond him. The hangar itself looked gigantic. Was he getting too close? The air buffeted about the open cockpit. The machine shook so much that it was hard to see clearly. He quickly pulled at the final toggle and hoped he wasn't too late. And still no towering burst of flames. Why couldn't he see where the bombs had fallen? Had they gone through the roof or the side and burst inside? They must have burst somewhere. And then, as he pulled out, he felt the shock of the explosion of a bomb.

Something caught Babington's eye beyond the right-hand end of the hangar roof. It must have been one of the machine-gun platforms they had been told about. He twisted round. Yes! Halfway along the hangar there was a hole in the roof! But where were the flames? There weren't any flames! 'Pull up, pull up you bloody fool!' He pulled back on the control stick. The nose came up and the lower wing blocked out the view below. Straight ahead over the nose of the machine the open country came into view again, and a little to the right but close ahead there was a slightly raised circular platform. There was a gun on it – probably some sort of pom-pom. It was firing. Babington was now not much above, if not actually below, the roof level of the big hangar behind him. Instinctively he slewed to the left – thought better of it, and straightened out again. He was near to panic. 'Keep down – keep going you dammed fool! They can't fire into the hangar.' He then found that in his hand he was holding his Mauser pistol. This filled him with confidence. As he streaked past, laughing like a fool – he let rip at the men on the platform. 'That'll larn 'em.' Doubtless he hit nothing, but it felt good and he flew close enough to see that he had scared them, that they couldn't get their gun to bear upon him.

His engine was still whirling madly round and appeared momentarily to have taken on a new lease of life. Everything suddenly seemed so much quieter. His aircraft sounded and felt all right. He couldn't see any holes in it. He was clear!

He screwed his head around again to see what was happening behind him. There was no more firing and there was only a misty, drifting confusion of smoke. Keeping low, he flew straight on for a bit and then swung slowly round, left towards Lake Constance. Over the lake once more – how still and placid it all looked – he turned right climbing gradually and headed westwards on his way back to the French frontier and Belfort. Babington reflected that even if they hadn't left the great hangar in an inferno of flaming gas, things hadn't gone too badly. He was certain that he had hit it. It had been impossible to miss it. Maybe the gas bags of the Zeppelin inside had not been filled. The airship might have been completely wrecked without being burnt. Anyhow, they had done their best.

Meanwhile, unknown to the aviators, on the ground the Germans made some effort to make up for the surprise that the planes had inflicted upon them. News of the raid was telegraphed from town to town on the likely route home. The Swiss border was closely watched to see whether they crossed the frontier. One source says that 'Motor cars mounting machine guns and anti-aircraft cannon were dispatched at full speed to the most likely points.'[11] However unlikely this may sound to us, the raiders were only flying at around 60 mph and it would take almost two hours before they left German territory. But the two remaining aircraft crossed the Rhine unmolested.

It was colder than ever as Babington droned on along the length of the lake. His engine was alright but even now with no bombs and half the petrol gone, it wasn't giving as much power as it should. It seemed a long time before the end of the lake came in sight. At this speed it was going to take some time to cover the next stretch to where the Rhine ran roughly due north – where he must cross and where his map ended. When, at length, the Rhine came in sight the sun was getting lower. Directly below the machine the visibility was still good, but in the distance, and particularly ahead to westward, a thin ground mist slurred the contours and made it difficult to pick up distant landmarks.

On the outward journey, he had tried to memorise the landmarks as he had crossed the Rhine. Nothing that he could see now chimed with his memory. Now, at the point where he thought he should be crossing the Rhine, he turned on to the reciprocal course that he had noted down over three hours before. That should take him straight to Belfort. As he advanced off his map and peered anxiously through his oil-smeared goggles into the deteriorating visibility, it became increasingly obvious to him that he was lost. He had come so far and was surely so close to base and yet … Turning first this way and then that to try and find something that he recognised from his outward flight, he finally accepted that he had better get down while he could still see possible landing sites on the ground.

And so it was, virtually out of fuel, and by his own calculations well overdue, that he found himself in a field with his pistol in one hand and his lighter in the other ready to torch his aircraft.

Presently an elderly farmer with a pitchfork appeared accompanied by a boy. Babington beckoned him on, shouting 'Anglais'. Leaving the boy by the hedge, the farmer advanced cautiously. Babington couldn't understand a word he said, but soon the man was beaming amiably. He thumped the ground with his pitchfork and shouted 'La France'. Babington got back into the machine, turned off the petrol and collected his papers. He was down somewhere in France. In fact he was at Vesoul some 30 miles to the south-west of Belfort. A gendarme and more people appeared. He left the machine in the care of the gendarme and went off in a farm cart to a telephone in the post office of the local hamlet.

After a meal of bread, omelette and absinthe, followed by more absinthe, Babington was collected and returned to Belfort. Here he heard that Briggs had been shot down and he realised that when he had seen the men converging on an aircraft, he had, in fact, watched Briggs being captured. He was glad that he hadn't tried to attack him.

Late that night, Babington and Sippe fell deeply asleep, with the sound of their engines still throbbing in their ears, and with the intention of having another attempt at the Zeppelin sheds on the morrow before the defences were beefed up. But it was not to be. The following day the weather broke and the team received their recall orders.

Ironically, of the aircraft involved, Briggs's machine, which was shot down with him at Friedrichshafen, was to have the longest service life of the four involved in the raid – the Germans repaired it and it was seen in German markings in 1917. Sippe's plane failed to return from another raid three months later; the pilot was killed. Babington's machine crashed, injuring the pilot, in June the following year and was written off. Shepherd's and subsequently Cannon's machine lasted a little longer but seems to have been jinxed. In June 1915, it was landed in a bog in mistake for the aerodrome and damaged. Ten days later it was shot down by 'friendly fire' near Canvey Island. In October 1915, its undercarriage was damaged in a bombing practice and it was damaged twice more, once in a ground collision with another aircraft, before it was finally disposed of in 1916.

Notwithstanding their professed concerns about security, the French made quite a fuss of the pilots and awarded all three of them the Legion d'Honour. Sippe and Babington received theirs in a parade in the hangar. All three were also immediately awarded the Distinguished Service Order. Briggs received his medals when he escaped from captivity from a train a couple of years later, and he was to win a second Distinguished Service Order before the war was finished. It would be difficult to improve upon the summary of the British Official Historian, Sir Walter Raleigh, who wrote:

> The pilots deserve all praise for their admirable navigation, and the machines must not be forgotten. There have since been many longer and greater raids, but this flight of 250 miles, into gunfire, across enemy country, in the frail little Avro and its humble horsepower, can compare as an achievement with the best of them, and some part of the credit must be spared for those who planned it and for those who tended and prepared the machines. The men on the ground or in the engine room, or in the racing stable, who have no part in the excitement and renown of action, are the invisible creators of victory.

Churchill's announcement of the raid in Parliament caused a stir. British euphoria about it was inversely related to British anxiety about Zeppelins and this raid did something to deplete further the aura of invincibility of these airships.

The pilots experienced a great sense of anti-climax. They had seen smoke and had felt the concussion of their bombs, but they had been expecting and hoping for something much more spectacular. They all had Marix's explosion at Düsseldorf in their minds and wondered why they hadn't produced the same result. They had after all dropped up to eleven bombs to Marix's two.

Pemberton Billing had already heard from his contact in Switzerland who had reported seeing, from Romanshorn across Lake Constance, flames of considerable magnitude issuing from the Zeppelin factory. Further 'news' soon filtered in. On 27 November, a French newspaper reported that, in spite of information to the contrary from German sources, 'the news is confirmed that a Zeppelin was completely destroyed.'[12]

A Swiss engineer, who is said to have witnessed the bombardment from a hotel near the Zeppelin plant, stated that while nine bombs fell in an area around the shed throwing up much debris, two bombs fell on the main shed and greatly damaged a Zeppelin. The hydrogen gas works nearby was also destroyed, exploding with gigantic flames up into the sky. This engineer said that an atmosphere of panic apparently set in on Friedrichshafen. 'A great network construction has been built above the Zeppelin sheds to guard against future aeroplane raids,' he said, and a considerable increase of the defences by way of men and anti-aircraft guns was immediately put in hand.

It is this report from Geneva dated 1 December 1914 which has informed British historiography.[13] We don't know who the Swiss engineer was or anything about the nature of his connection with the British authorities. But it is his account that forms the basis of the official history written in 1922, and virtually every other history ever since. A Swiss assembly worker, Albert Rieser, was convicted of espionage and was sentenced to eight years jail.[14] Was he the 'Swiss engineer'? Was he Pemberton Billing's contact? If so, the information he passed on was fantasy.

The truth is rather less dramatic. The internal daily situation report for 21 November of the Zeppelin construction company tells a different story. After setting out the status of the airships under construction and giving the reports from the various parts of the site, a note is added at the bottom.[15] It describes how at around midday three 'English' planes attacked the construction shed. Seven bombs were dropped and one came through the roof. It notes that one flyer, Briggs, was shot down and that 'Materialschaden entstanden: Keiner' – there was no damage to any materials.

There could be no more authoritative source than this contemporary, routine, humble, internal management tool. This is confirmed by the report of a certain Weymann, possibly the commander of one of the Zeppelins in the shed, to his master, Hans von Schiller. He wrote that one bomb, apparently dropped by Sippe, went into a magazine but it didn't explode. Another, if it had gone another 60 feet, would have destroyed his airship. As it was, his Zeppelin was unscratched and the bomb merely blew out the windows of the shed.[16] He reported no other damage. There is even a hand-drawn map in his report indicating where the bombs landed. This report from a man who had no reason to do anything other than explain faithfully to his master what had happened to the assets under his command must also be given its due credence.

The German military authorities would have known from the Pemberton Billing incident that someone had conducted a close-in reconnaissance. There was also a number of rumours of espionage reported in the local press. It was said that a broken-down car with two men had been seen not far from Friedrichshafen on 4 November. An official of the Zeppelin works is supposed to have identified Briggs as one of the men. The British ambassador in Switzerland was suspected of having used a holiday to do a recce. He was supposed to have crossed into Germany on false documents and climbed a church tower with another younger man. This was apparently denied by the Swiss government.

Murray Sueter also pays tribute to 'a gallant Canadian officer', Colonel Grant Morden, who 'obtained at much personal risk … very valuable information of a secret nature'. Morden was a very wealthy financier with diverse business interests. One can only speculate upon the nature of his contribution, but perhaps it arose from his many and various international commercial contacts.[17]

There were casualties, however. According to the local newspaper, the *Seeblatt*, a house nearby was damaged, windows were blown out and a 21-year-old Swiss unmarried tailor's assistant was killed immediately by a splinter to the heart. The wife of an engine driver was badly hurt in the head and arm, and another lady, Fraulein Mugg, lost her arm.[18]

It is in these everyday local journals written for the consumption of local people, far away from official histories, that one gathers a real sense of what happens in war. Notwithstanding any unnamed casualties that might have been incurred by the German Zeppelin raids on Liège and Antwerp, or the British bombing raids on Cologne and Düsseldorf, these people – Fraulein Mugg, a young tailor's assistant, and the wife of an engine driver – were probably the first civilian air-raid casualties in history. It is immaterial whether they were injured by British bombs or by falling shrapnel from the numerous shells that were fired at all three aircraft. They were to be a melancholy harbinger.

What is quite clear is that the raid had no perceptible effect on Germany's ability to manufacture Zeppelins, although this demonstration of their vulnerability did cause the Germans to rethink entirely their assumptions. Much effort was expended in establishing an effective anti-aircraft defence, and they were persuaded to establish a second construction centre in Potsdam, out of the likely range of British aircraft.

Friedrichshafen was not attacked again by the British in the First World War. The Swiss complaint about the alleged breach of their neutrality may have contributed to this but this is unlikely to have deterred Churchill, who is said to have advised the Foreign Office to 'tell the Swiss to go and milk their cows'; advice which was not taken. More likely causes were the onset of winter weather and the knowledge that surprise had been lost. By the time spring came round, Churchill and the Admiralty had their minds on other theatres.

The French were not so constrained and they conducted a number of minor raids right through to October 1918. None of these raids was any more successful than the first raid, although they served the purpose of forcing the German authorities to install increasingly effective and costly anti-aircraft defences. However, all this was an insignificant bagatelle when compared to the terrible devastation that was rained down on the town by the British and the Americans in 1943 and 1944 during the Second World War.

On the day after the raid, the pilots watched Pemberton Billing set off for home at his usual high speed. Sippe and Babington followed in a borrowed car which needed to be returned to Paris. About 60 miles down the road, on a patch of ice on a snow-covered road, they came across the last of the white racing car – it had skidded off the road, back-end on, into a poplar tree.

Noel Pemberton Billing received no official recognition for his key part in this operation, but he went on to become a very well-known public figure. He contested and lost the parliamentary seat of Mile End in 1915, but won East Hertford as an independent the following year. Thereafter he became a controversial right-wing independent Member, setting himself up as a self-appointed goad to those in authority responsible for air matters and an advocate for a single air service. He held the seat until 1921 and was succeeded by none other than his old boss, Murray Sueter.

Notes

1 Burt, R.A., *British Battleships of World War One*, Arms and Armour Press, 1986, p. 186.

2 Ballantyne, Iain, *Warspite: Warships of the Royal Navy*, Leo Cooper, 2001, p. 27.

3 Marder, Arthur, *From the Dreadnought to Scapa Flow*, vol. I, *The Road to War 1904–1914*, OUP, 1961, p. 405.

4 Liddell Hart, Basil, *History of the First World War*, Book Club Associates in arrangement with Cassell & Co, 1970, p. 587.

5 Stoney, Barbara, *Twentieth Century Maverick: The Life of Noel Pemberton Billing*, Bank House Books 2004, p. 15.

6 Principal sources for this account of the Friedrichshafen Raid are Babington, John, *A 1914 Naval Air Affair*, from the papers of Mrs Penelope Willis, 1962, edited by Dr Norman Lyne, and Royal Naval Air Service Operational Reports 1914, ADM 116/1352 at the Public Record Office, Kew.

7 Jones, Neville, *The Origins of Strategic Bombing*, William Kimber, 1973, p. 74.

8 Rennles, Keith, *Independent Force: The War Diary of the Daylight Squadrons of the Independent Air Force June–November 1918*, Grub Street, 2002, p. 9.

9 Stoney, *Twentieth Century Maverick*, p. 74.

10 Bleibler, Jürgen, *Luftkrieg über Friedrichshafen 1914-1918*, Zeppelin Museum Friedrichshafen Wissenschaftliches Jahrbuch, 2001.

11 Wood, Eric, *Thrilling Deeds of British Airmen*, Harrap, 1917, p. 42.

12 Royal Naval Air Service Operational Reports 1914, ADM 116/1352 at the Public Record Office, Kew

13 Ibid.

14 Bleibler, *Luftkrieg über Friedrichshafen 1914-1918*.

15 Tagesbericht vom Samstag, den 21. November 1914. Paper LZA 3/6, Archiv der Luftschiffbau GmbH, Friedrichshafen.

16 Bleibler, *Luftkrieg über Friedrichshafen 1914-1918*. This is possibly the same man who is referred to by Douglas Robinson in *The Zeppelin in Combat*, Foulis & Co., 1971, p. 43.

17 Grant Morden became MP for Brentford and Chiswick, and died a bankrupt in 1932.

18 Bleibler, *Luftkrieg über Friedrichshafen 1914-1918*.

Chapter 5

Cuxhaven – The First Carrier Strike

Aircraft offered a means for navies to extend their striking power a long way beyond the reach of their guns. However, in 1914, most navies depended upon land bases for their aircraft. The German capture of Antwerp in October 1914, and the invasion of much of Belgium and Northern France, put the known Zeppelin sheds out of range of British land-based aircraft, although the use of Belfort to launch the raid on Friedrichshafen was one stratagem which overcame this problem of lack of reach. There would come a time when Zeppelins would be based in Belgium, and this would put their sheds within the reach again of Royal Naval Air Service aircraft based at Dunkirk. But long before this, men were devising other ways to extend the range of aircraft so that they could strike beyond the range of ships' guns, and the endurance of early aircraft engines.

From the very beginning of the war, minds had been engaged on finding ways to strike at the base of the German Fleet in Wilhelmshaven. The Battle of Heligoland at the end of August 1914 had been part of an attempt to entice German warships into a trap. The difficulty for surface ships was that, in trying to lay an ambush for the Germans, they might themselves fall victim to a counter-trap sprung by submarines or motor torpedo boats. However, if aircraft could somehow carry the strike weapon, this difficulty would be minimised. The German base was a long way beyond the range of any aircraft, but if aircraft could be carried closer to the target in a ship, then all sorts of possibilities might open up.

Much had been learned from exercising with the light fleet cruiser HMS *Hermes* which had been taken in hand as a seaplane carrier in 1913 for that year's summer fleet exercises. The concept behind her conversion to seaplane carrier was to give the fleet an improved observation capability, similar to that provided by the Zeppelin to the Germans. The whole complex routine of embarking aircraft, stowing and servicing them inside their canvas hangars, hoisting them over the side without damaging them, starting them while on the water, and recovering them again – all this had to be learned, practised, relearned and practised again. This valuable experience was gathered before HMS *Hermes* went into refit in August 1914. She was sunk soon after coming out of refit, but in a sense she had already performed her greatest service as the experimental and training base which inspired the purchase of three cross-Channel ferries, *Engadine*, *Riviera* and *Empress*, which were converted into seaplane tenders. All the lessons learned from the *Hermes* were applied to these new acquisitions

But no matter how much the Navy practised and worked out drills, and developed equipment to match the tasks, they found that launching and recovering seaplanes was never going to be a slick operation. Ships had to stop dead in the water for perhaps an hour or so in order to hoist the seaplanes over the side, and again to recover them. This made them and their aircraft especially vulnerable to U-boat attack or unpleasant surprises in some other form. It was a highly weather-dependent exercise and even in good weather, there was no guarantee that the aircraft would actually take off. A flat calm presented almost as much difficulty as a rough sea because the aircraft had to generate enough power and lift to break the surface suction. The early seaplanes sometimes did not develop enough of either. With a bomb load, or an observer on board, or both an observer and bombs, take-off became even more uncertain. So from the earliest days, men wondered how they might overcome all these limitations. *Hermes* had been fitted with a flying-off deck from which a small seaplane mounted on a wheeled trolley could be launched; at the end of its flight, the plane had to land on the water and be hoisted in. At the same time, the Admiralty was considering the idea of a flat-topped ship from which wheeled aircraft might take off and on which they could land without the necessity of stopping the ship, but this would not take material form for some time to come. Meanwhile, the only aircraft capable of operating at sea were seaplanes.

Seaplanes had only been in existence since 1910, but taking off and landing on the water was by now routinely practised. As with military aviation, it was envisaged that the seaplane's chief role would be reconnaissance, and it was with this in mind that the *Engadine*, *Riviera* and *Empress* had been procured and converted.

However, Churchill had other ideas. Always believing that offence was the best form of defence, and determined to destroy the Zeppelins on the ground if he couldn't as yet bring them down in the air, he decided that the ferries should be used as part of his campaign to bomb the Zeppelin sheds in Belgium and Germany. Instead of joining the Grand Fleet in Scotland, these ships were sent to join the naval force based in Harwich. The Harwich Force chiefly comprised destroyers and cruisers, and its task was to 'mind' the southern part of the North Sea. It was commanded by Commodore Reginald Tyrwhitt. The other force at Harwich was the Eighth Submarine Flotilla and this was commanded by Commodore Roger Keyes.

Notwithstanding the overall unreadiness of the Royal Navy for a world war in 1914, it harboured at least its fair share of able, aggressive, talented men and was open minded enough to give them sea room. David Beatty was one of these men. An admiral before his thirty-ninth birthday, he commanded the main battle cruiser force from 1913 until 1916, and he and his ships were to be found in the vanguard of all the significant dreadnought actions in home waters during the first two years of war. Beatty was not on centre stage during the Cuxhaven Raid but he and his able but more cautious master, Admiral John Jellicoe, featured nevertheless. At the end of 1916, at the age of forty-five, Beatty took over from Jellicoe and became the Commander-in-Chief of the Grand Fleet, the most powerful fleet in history to that date.

Beatty may have been an exception in exercising high command while so young, but he was not alone in having a reputation as an aggressive naval commander. Reginald Tyrwhitt, a year older than Beatty, and Roger Keyes, a year younger than him, were also remarkable men who played a most important part at sea in the First World War. They were both destined to achieve the highest naval rank, and to be successful influential officers in peace and war, but their careers were not rocket assisted like Beatty's. Tyrwhitt and Keyes, and Britain, were unfortunate in that they were too young to exercise high command at sea in this war, and too old to do so in the next one.

Tyrwhitt stayed in command of the Harwich Force throughout the war and commanded it with the greatest distinction. His ships saw the first action of the war when they sank a German minelayer on the first day of hostilities, 5 August. He and Keyes had planned the Heligoland battle later that month where, backed up by Beatty's battlecruisers, they sank three German cruisers. No part of the Royal Navy was to be more constantly in the front line throughout the war than Tyrwhitt and his cruisers and destroyers.

Keyes was to become the Chief of Staff in the Dardanelles. He, like Tyrwhitt, Beatty and Churchill himself, never missed a chance to attack, and there were some who thought that if Keyes had been the commander, rather than the Chief of Staff, at the Dardanelles, the outcome of the naval campaign in that theatre might have been rather different. But it wasn't to be. After command of a battleship, and then a spell as the Director of Naval Plans, he was to command the Dover Patrol, which was a vital player in the defeat of the German U-boat campaign. It was in this role that he planned and led the Zeebrugge Raid in 1918, a raid which was to draw on the lessons of the Dardanelles, and which itself was to become the inspiration for many raids and other amphibious operations since.

All these men were seized with the importance of naval aviation. Indeed, Beatty it was who foresaw the day when an admiral, rather than command the battle from a dreadnought, would go to war based in a ship carrying aeroplanes. But that was still some way in the future. Meanwhile Keyes and Tyrwhitt, two birds of a feather, were to be responsible for planning and executing the Cuxhaven Raid.

There were several abortive attempts to attack the Zeppelin hangars at Cuxhaven. The first attack was planned for 24 October 1914, but the weather quickly deteriorated to such an extent that take-off was not even attempted. The Navy, and Harwich Force in particular, had many balls in the air at this time and the weather was not the only complicating factor. To designate and co-ordinate the participation of a substantial number of ships and submarines from their many other tasks was no small matter, but another attempt was made a month later at the end of November, two days after the attack on Friedrichshafen.

This time, it was a subsidiary part of a much larger operation involving Admiral Jellicoe and the Grand Fleet. There was a whiff of 'mixed missions' about the operation. The Admiralty advised Jellicoe that the carrier operation would be a good opportunity for him to try and bring elements of the German High Seas Fleet to battle on terms of his choosing. Jellicoe certainly saw that as the primary aim. The aviation element of the operation was to be something of a tethered goat. Tyrwhitt went ahead believing that the primary aim was to strike the airship hangars, and set off to deploy his forces accordingly. However, second thoughts about the safety of the goat seem to have smitten Jellicoe at the last minute and the aviation element of the operation was cancelled. The attempt to lure out the German fleet with destroyers and cruisers went ahead without success. The only visible reaction was an attack by one German seaplane from the base on the island of Heligoland which bombed, but missed, a British cruiser. With the benefit of hindsight, this was always going to be the most likely result.

No plan survives first contact with the enemy and, when men in battle are presented with unforeseen circumstances – which they always will be – they must have the clearest idea what the overall goal of an operation is so that, in a dynamic situation, they can take decisions which support their higher commander's intention. If there is clarity and unity of mission, everybody is pulling on the same rope in the same direction and can act accordingly. Dual aims, or mixed missions, in any military operation tend to lead to confusion of priorities and often end up with neither goal being achieved successfully. That is what happened on this occasion. If the goal had simply been enticement, then the tethered goat should have been deployed where it was most enticing, and the Grand Fleet would doubtless have been placed in a position where it could destroy any German ships coming after the tethered goat – preferably before they killed the goat. But Tyrwhitt's plan of striking the airship sheds turned out to be incompatible with Jellicoe's, and so Tyrwhitt's operation was called off at the last moment. This flaw of mixed missions was to beset most of the operations to tempt the German High Seas Fleet out of it bases and ambush it, and none of them ever really succeeded.

The next attack on Zeppelin sheds was set well in advance, for 25 December. Why that date was chosen three weeks ahead is not known, except that it was probable that at least some elements of the Imperial High Seas Fleet would be at a lower state of readiness on that day. That being so, it is a little surprising that yet another enticing element was built into this, the third attempt. The weather certainly couldn't be predicted that far in advance and so the operation was always going to be contingent on the chance of decent weather.

The Grand Fleet would once more deploy and lurk at a distance in the hope of ambushing any elements of the High Seas Fleet that might sally forth. But this time, instead of depending on the surface fleet for protection, which almost certainly would have arrived too late, Roger Keyes and his submarines would provide close support.

Sueter's directive to Tyrwhitt and Keyes is a model of clarity.[1] Only a page long, it acknowledges the difficulty of co-ordinating a large body of ships and synchronising their movements with the doubtful prospect of good weather. For this reason Tyrwhitt was given instructions to conduct a stand-alone operation with his own cruisers and destroyers, with Keyes' submarines in support. The aim of the operation was unambiguously laid out as the destruction of the Cuxhaven airship sheds. Sueter then allocated subsidiary reconnaissance tasks for the aircraft of each ship, but only once 'all machines' had dropped their bombs on the sheds. Each of the three ships, HMS *Empress*, *Riviera* and *Engadine*, would carry three aircraft, and each aircraft would carry three 20lb Hales bombs, 'it having been proved that one of these bombs will destroy a Zeppelin in a shed', presumably referring to the results of the Düsseldorf raid, and what at the time were believed to be the results of the Friedrichshafen raid.

Up to a relatively late juncture, confusion seems to have existed in the Admiralty about precisely what they were going to attack, and where it was. What were referred to as the airship sheds at Cuxhaven, and indeed have been referred to as such ever since, were in fact 8 miles south of Cuxhaven and 3 miles inland, near the town of Nordholz. It appears that this fact only became known in the Admiralty in December, which gives little grounds for believing that either of the previous operations, if they had gone ahead, would have been successful. Sueter's orders state that 'it is known that one airship shed has been built at Cuxhaven, 10 miles inland; recent report states that four Zeppelins are now at this place, so probably the station has been added to.'[2]

But Nordholz was indeed a worthy target – it had recently become the headquarters for the Naval Airship Division of the Imperial German Navy. Eventually, it would be become a substantial base with a number of hangars, but even in 1914 it boasted some significant infrastructure. This included some barracks, and facilities for manufacturing and storing hydrogen gas. Of greatest importance, however, was the newly constructed double hangar, each hangar 600 feet long, 100 feet wide, and nearly 120 feet high. The hangars were mounted side by side on a single revolving turntable which allowed Zeppelins to be deployed in and out regardless of the direction of the wind. They were of the most advanced design and were the first hangars to be constructed in this way. The only other sheds capable of basing Zeppelins operating in the North Sea were two fixed hangars at Fuhlsbüttel near Hamburg. Destruction of the Nordholz sheds could therefore have crippled the German Navy's Zeppelin operational capability.

Perhaps acknowledging that intelligence on the sheds' location was weak, and the possibility of doubtful weather, Sueter directed that if the sheds were not found, 'they are to attack the enemy's ships or any positions of military importance and endeavour to destroy them'.

Plainly Sueter took Tyrwhitt's ideas and wishes into account before he issued his directive because, while Tyrwhitt's detailed orders to his squadron of cruisers, destroyers and carriers are dated 2 December, Sueter's are dated 18 December. This is not necessarily a case of putting the cart before the horse, but rather a useful clarification and authorisation of what might have already been agreed verbally.

Keyes' orders to his ten submarines stated that their objectives were 'to attack any vessels which may come out to engage the squadron' and 'to pick up the pilots of any of the seaplanes which may be unable to reach the squadron'.[3] Detailed instructions were given to tow stranded seaplanes towards their mother ships, and if forced to abandon them, at least to try and salvage the engines before destroying the plane. At least three of the submarines had subsidiary tasks which involved them sitting on the surface to provide a navigation mark for the seaplanes. Moreover, if they saw a ship that they could not attack, they were to surface and send a warning message to other friendly vessels. A modern submariner might arch his eyebrow at such a variety of tasks, most of which might distract him from the task that submarines are best at, namely hunting unseen and destroying enemy vessels of every description. This was another case of mixed missions. No priority between them was offered and one wonders which of these missions was uppermost in the mind of the planners when the deployment locations of the submarines were chosen, and what would have happened if a submarine commander had been forced to choose between two, or even three, concurrent missions. But submarine warfare was almost as new as maritime air warfare and this was the first time that either had been conducted for real by the Royal Navy. The underwater performance of these early submarines was fairly limited. They tended to stay on the surface so long as it was deemed safe to do so, and so they operated more like submersible torpedo boats rather than submarines as we understand them.

All submarines were to have a broad red and white chequered stripe painted round the conning tower to identify them as friendly. All aircraft were to have a large red circle painted under their wings together with a Union Jack.

As well as Keyes and Tyrwhitt, there were other remarkable men involved in this operation, some of whom were to have chequered careers. Lieutenant Commander Martin Nasmith, who commanded one of Keyes' submarines, was to earn himself a Victoria Cross the following year in the Dardanelles. Flight Commander Frederick Bowhill, who commanded the *Empress*, was to become an air chief marshal in the Royal Air Force, and command Coastal Command and Ferry Command during the Second World War. Perhaps the most widely known personality was Erskine Childers. Childers, one time clerk in the House of Commons, soldier in the Boer War and highly skilled and experienced yachtsman, was now a lieutenant in the Royal Naval Volunteer Reserve. He was there by special request. In 1903, he had written and published an outstanding, best-selling spy thriller called *The Riddle of the Sands*, set among the intricate necklace of islands off the German North Sea coast. The hero of the book, also an exceptional sailor, discovered German preparations for mounting an invasion of Britain from the rivers and bays on the coast behind the islands. The book, a ripping yarn of the first degree and the ancestor of all subsequent spy thrillers, struck a chord with the British public just at a time when relations with Germany were worsening, and a naval base at Rosyth was being built to take account of the changed strategic circumstances. However improbable Childers' plot might have been, no one had a better first-hand knowledge of the remote, labyrinthine shallows and eddies of the Frisian Coast. Rather like Ewen Southby-Tailyour, who had sailed extensively in the waters around the Falkland Islands before 1982, and who became an invaluable source of information when it came to recapturing them, so Childers made his knowledge and experience available for the sailors and pilots on this operation.

The captain of the *Engadine*, Squadron Commander Cecil L'Estrange Malone, makes especial mention of Erskine Childers' contribution in his operational report.[4] Having freely given of his knowledge in the planning, he then flew with Flight Commander Cecil Kilner, formerly a captain in the Royal Marine Light Infantry, as his observer, and again Malone acknowledges his contribution to the success of Kilner's reconnaissance flight. On this raid, Kilner was to win the first of the two Distinguished Service Orders he was to be awarded during the war. Childers went on to have a distinguished career in the Royal Naval Air Service at home and in the Gallipoli campaign, and was awarded the Distinguished Service Cross. He finished the war as a major in the Royal Air Force, but was not destined to enjoy his fame for long. He was an ardent Irish nationalist and had already indulged in a bit of gun-running in his yacht in 1914. In 1919, he joined the Irish Republican Movement. An implacable believer in a united free Ireland, he was caught during the civil war by the Irish Free State forces with a gun on his person and was shot by firing squad in 1922.

Squadron Commander Malone himself became a colonel in the Royal Air Force before the end of the war. He then became a Coalition Liberal Member of Parliament. In 1919 he visited Russia as a journalist and became a deeply committed Communist and Britain's first Communist MP. In 1920, he argued in a speech that during the course of a workers' revolution it was reasonable to execute prominent members of the bourgeoisie. 'What are a few Churchills or Curzons on lampposts compared to the massacre of thousands of human beings?' he said. This landed him in jail for six months, his OBE was withdrawn, and he was struck off the Navy List. He then worked actively for affiliation of the Communist Party of Great Britain to the Labour Party, and eventually became a junior minister in Ramsay McDonald's administration in 1931.

Meanwhile, in 1914, Cecil Malone was already an experienced and noted aviator, and on this operation had tactical command of the carriers and the seaplanes. He issued clear and detailed instructions which reflected the clarity of Sueter's directive, laying down in detail what each aircraft should carry, including lifebelts – no parachutes – and the routines and timings for hoisting out seaplanes and preparing them for flight on the water. He set specific reconnaissance tasks but made clear that the main objective was to destroy the airship sheds. It too is a model of its kind in that it covers all the necessary detail and yet leaves the pilots sufficient freedom to react appropriately to unforeseen circumstances.

The planning probably benefited from the two aborted 'rehearsals'. Taken all together, the orders indicate it was a well-conceived and planned operation with clear objectives, and with sufficient flexibility to achieve secondary objectives if the primary one was to prove unachievable. This was just as well because in the event, none of the aircraft was to find the primary objective. The intelligence on the target was uncertain, but as good as they were likely to get. However, its precise location, before the age of aerial reconnaissance and satellite imagery, was always going to be problematical.

Another doubtful area was the part that the Grand Fleet might play if things got rough. Once again, the Grand Fleet never came closer than 100 miles to Heligoland Island and would have been too far away to help if the Harwich Force were to be attacked by superior forces without warning. But this time, with ten submarines in a screen in front of the Force, they were a far from helpless tethered goat.

In his excellent and authoritative account of the Cuxhaven Raid,[5] R.D. Layman points out that the Harwich Force with its seaplanes and submarines was the tip of a huge spear. Behind them, ready to pounce on any enemy ships that sortied out, were battleships and battlecruisers of the Grand Fleet. Perhaps 150 British warships were in the North Sea looking and hoping for a piece of the action. In truth, they weren't really in support of the Harwich Force. They were on what was effectively a separate operation, namely, to destroy any heavy German units that sortied out as a result of the Cuxhaven Raid. Nevertheless, the total of 81.5lb of explosives in the twenty-seven bombs carried by the seaplanes of the Harwich Force was the principal striking weapon of a huge flotilla. 'For the first time in the history of naval warfare, shipboard aircraft were to be the sole striking arm of a fleet'.

At 0500 hrs on Christmas Eve, two hours before dawn, the Harwich Force commanded by Commodore Tyrwhitt comprising the light cruisers *Arethusa* and *Undaunted*, and eight destroyers, all escorting the three seaplane carriers *Engadine*, *Empress* and *Riviera*, sailed from its base. The submarines together with the destroyers *Lurcher* and *Firedrake*, all commanded by Commodore Keyes, had deployed some twenty-four hours before.

The same day as Tyrwhitt sailed, a single German aeroplane dropped the first bomb on British soil. It flew from Belgium and the bomb landed in a garden near Dover Castle. It was the second attempt a bomb had been dropped in Dover Harbour on a similar raid the day before.[6]

Map 3 - Area of seaplane operations, 25 December 1914.

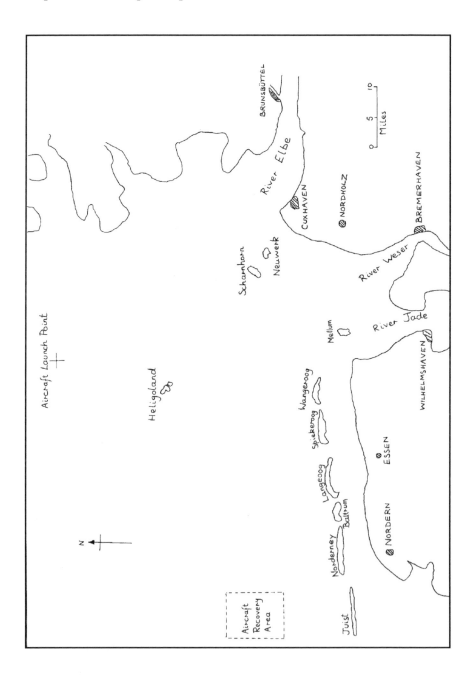

Twenty-five hours later, early on Christmas morning, the Harwich Force arrived at the point designated for the launch of the strike 10 miles north of Heligoland Island off the Schleswig-Holstein coast. The weather was perfect, but bitterly cold. A couple of hours earlier, they had encountered four small vessels showing trawlers' lights. One of them was heard to transmit what seemed to be a contact report. This elicited some seventeen messages in response from a radio station on Heligoland. It would have been strange if someone even as experienced and stout hearted as Tyrwhitt had not got the jitters at this moment. Here they were within 30 miles of the German coast and a couple of hour's sailing time away from the principal base of a fleet second only in power and strength to that of the Royal Navy; and it looked as if they had been discovered before they had even started. Ten submarines in front of him was no guarantee that enemy ships could not attack him. It needed only one of the many dreadnoughts that must be based there to come out and the cat would be among the pigeons. The Grand Fleet manoeuvring somewhere out in the middle of the North Sea could do nothing for them.

Sometimes an operation can generate a momentum which itself becomes a factor sufficient to influence whether the operation goes ahead or is aborted. This momentum can be such that it outweighs other factors which, in other circumstances, might stop the operation. For instance, the D-Day landings in 1944 were scheduled for 5 June. There were only three days in each month when the tide and moon met the many and various requirements of the diverse players. However, the weather was a wild card which could not be predicted far in advance. On the evening of 4 June, with all the ships, troops and aircraft in position to proceed with the landing, the weather was foul. Better weather was predicted for 6 June but it was far from certain. Eisenhower knew that men could not be kept cooped up in their ships for very long, and to halt or turn back the machinery would probably break it. In the midst of a gale on 4 June, with a hope and a prayer, he decided to go ahead regardless on 6 June.

Tyrwhitt, having seen two attempts aborted already, knew that it could be many weeks or months before the ships, the weather and the war might conspire to let him have another go. It would be too bad to have to turn back now. While he was pondering, a bright light was seen dead ahead low on the horizon. Was it a Zeppelin, or some kind of searchlight? As it slowly rose in the sky, getting brighter in the mist, the navigation officer twigged what it was. It was Venus. It was Christmas morning, after all, and here was the star in the East! That was enough for Tyrwhitt. Nothing would stop them now.[7]

Each seaplane carrier was mother to three seaplanes, all nine of them manufactured by Short Brothers. This company was formed in 1908, but the Short brothers, Horace, Eustace and Oswald, had started by selling balloons in 1902. Their long and fruitful association with naval aviation began when they built their first seaplane which Charles Samson flew in Portland harbour in 1912. They became well attuned to the needs of maritime aviation, and soon designed and patented the 'Folder'. The Folder was the name given to the Short Admiralty Type 81, which was the first aeroplane on which the wings could be folded back along the fuselage for ease of stowage on board ship. It was also a generic term for aircraft which had this capability. All the aircraft on this raid were 'Folders'. They were all fairly similar types, each with the upper wing extending beyond the lower wing, and each with two main floats and a tail float, with smaller floats at the end of the wings. All were two-seater biplanes, but the choice of whether to carry a second person seems to have been left to individual pilots. An extra person, if he knew what he was doing, could be very useful for observing, but since the main mission was bombing, five out of the nine pilots chose to fly alone, presumably to increase the likelihood that they would be able to take off on the water with a load of three bombs.

Empress carried three 'improved' versions of the Type 74, the original unimproved mark not having the folding-wing capability. It was powered by a 100 hp Gnome rotary engine, a slightly more powerful version of the engine that drove the aircraft on the Düsseldorf and Friedrichshafen raids. This gave it a speed of 65 mph and a maximum flight duration of five hours. It had a wingspan of 57 feet. Only eight were ever built.

Engadine carried three Type 81s, or Folders. The 81 had a 160 hp Gnome rotary engine with a maximum speed of 78 mph. It was a bigger plane with a wingspan of 67 feet and was designed to carry torpedoes but it was never used in this role in war. Only five were ever built.

Riviera carried one Improved Type 74 and the only two Type 135s that were ever constructed. The Type 135 was a slightly smaller upgraded version of the Type 81. One of them had a 135 hp Salmson radial engine, and the other a 200 hp engine from the same manufacturer. Top speed was about 80 mph and they were the most advanced seaplanes of their day.

The squadron of ships arrived at the rendezvous on time at 0600 hrs. It was still dark, although the weather remained fine. The aircrews had exercised fully their privilege of having a free choice of what to eat for breakfast – most of them settled for huge quantities of the usual eggs and bacon with all the trimmings, including potted grouse. The temperature was around freezing and a thin film of ice had formed on exposed wet surfaces. It only took a short time to get all the planes slung out over the sides of their ships and into the water. Now they had to unfold the wings. This was done by mechanics with the aid of small boats, and by standing on the aircraft floats, which, although a practised routine, must always have been only for the nimble and sure of foot. It was getting lighter by now but the still rather poor light would not have made it any easier. Everything was ready shortly before 0700, when it was light enough to start flying. The order was given to start engines. This was always an uncertain evolution and the bitter cold would not have helped. Malone's plan was that the slower seaplanes, the Type 74s and Type 135s, would take off first and get a head start. One by one the mechanics on the floats swung the propellers, but none of the engines started straightaway.

The official reports are pretty matter of fact when describing this moment, but there cannot have been much that was matter of fact about it at the time. Rather, it must have been a highly charged, loaded few minutes. The carriers were all stopped dead in the water. Floating hard by were nine aircraft with their mechanics in their gigs and small craft all fussing about them, their engines obdurately inert. In the gathering light, it was bitterly cold, and men's fingers, and their nerves, must have been sorely tested. They believed they had been discovered. They were at their most vulnerable to attack from submarine, aircraft or surface craft of any kind. The appearance of the enemy in any shape or form now would demand some very difficult decisions and could seriously dislocate the operation. They could do nothing quickly, and aircraft and men would probably have to be abandoned.

The aircraft engines at last began to respond to the labours of their mechanics, and cough and splutter into life. First one, then three, then six aircraft were ready for take-off. Three engines persistently refused to start. In desperation, two mechanics, Chief Petty Officer Wright and Air Mechanic Kent, dived into the freezing water, fully clothed and without lifejackets, and swam to one aircraft to do what was necessary. They succeeded in getting Flight Lieutenant Edmonds' Type 74 machine running. Seven aircraft, after a long run-up, eventually heaved themselves into the air and set off on their way. Nothing that anyone could do could bring life to the engines of Flight Lieutenant Bone's Type 74 or Flight Commander Gaskell's Type 81. At 0720 hrs, seeing smoke rising from the direction of Heligoland and, having stayed five minutes longer than he had planned, Malone decided to cut his losses and gave the order to lift the two dead seaplanes back on board. By 0730, no doubt with alternate sighs of disappointment and relief, they were on their way.

The intention now was for the squadron to steer a circuitous route to the West, to a point where they could pick up the returning seaplanes after about three hours. They got away just in time because a Zeppelin was sighted within a few minutes coming from the direction of Heligoland Island. A short time later, a German seaplane was sighted in the same direction. Neither approached the force but since German seaplanes did not carry radios, it presumably disappeared back to Heligoland to deliver a contact report. Contrary to the belief of Tyrwhitt, this was in fact the first contact report received by the Germans that day. The trawlers they had seen earlier were probably just that – trawlers – and whatever radio transmission the British had picked up, they were not contact reports.

The German naval air arm reacted swiftly. Shortly *Empress*, which had trouble keeping up with the rest of the force due to inferior coal, was attacked by two seaplanes and a Zeppelin. In his report, Tyrwhitt made rather light of this attack. He said that, given ordinary sea room, he was convinced that ships had nothing to fear from seaplanes or Zeppelins. But it was not his ship that had been bombed. The captain of the *Empress*, Flight Commander Bowhill, whose ship had been bombed, put a quite different slant on it.

The ship was attacked by two German seaplanes of a type similar to the Shorts he had just deployed. The first one came in from the starboard bow at 2,000 feet and dropped six bombs all of which landed 200 to 300 yards away. The second aircraft came in from the port bow at 1,800 feet and dropped two larger bombs which straddled the ship. The bombs landed between 20 and 40 feet away and shook the ship severely. *Empress* was, after all, simply an unarmoured converted Channel ferry, and if one of these bombs had hit, who knows what might have happened. The crew were armed with rifles and kept up steady volleys of fire while Bowhill kept changing course throughout the attacks. But one is left with a sense that this attack, one of the first attempts to bomb a British ship while under way, was pressed home with skill and courage in the face of volleys of rifle fire, and was very nearly successful.

Soon afterwards, *Empress* was attacked by Zeppelin *L6* operating out from the very airship base that the British seaplanes had set off to destroy. This airship approached at about 5,000 feet and then, lining herself up above and in the same direction as the ship, came down to 2,000 feet. She appeared to drop a tracer bomb to give herself a line to go on, and then three bombs each of about 100lb. They all missed, but only by about 40 to 50 yards astern. She also opened up with a machine gun but to no great effect. Bowman undoubtedly improved his chances of survival by watching the rudders of the Zeppelin and anticipating its turn by throwing his own wheel over in the opposite direction. In spite of the limited manoeuvrability of the Zeppelin, it still seemed to drop its bombs with a fair degree of accuracy. Meanwhile, Bowman's sailors kept up a steady fusillade of rifle fire at the airship. With no tracer, it was impossible to adjust fire and there was no sign of any damage being inflicted, but it must have been akin to shooting at an ocean liner at a range of 700 yards – rather difficult to miss.

The other British ships now turned to back to the assistance of the lagging *Empress*. Using 6-inch shrapnel fired at extreme elevation, they persuaded the Zeppelin that she had had all the fun she was going to get for now, and she rose into the clouds and disappeared. Although she was later reported to have crashed-landed in the sea, the Zeppelin was in fact hardly damaged and returned home to Nordholz with only a few bullets holes in her gas bags.[8]

Meanwhile, as the Zeppelin *L6* was doing battle with the *Empress*, seven British seaplanes were trying to seek out and destroy its base.

Flight Commander Robert Ross took off in his Type 81 at 0710 hrs and, on his way to the coast, saw the same Zeppelin that the ships had seen in the vicinity of Heligoland Island. He was tempted to attack it but he was at 2,000 feet and it was at 4,000 feet, and he didn't think his machine would get up to her. In any case, Zeppelins were particularly good at ascending quickly, so the chances that he would catch this one were next to nil. He stuck to his main mission and carried on heading for the sheds. Shortly afterwards, he saw a second Zeppelin even higher at 5,000 feet. He also saw a number of ships, one of which shot at him and missed, but more importantly, ahead over land was a heavy bank of thick fog. He entered the bank on course for the sheds but visibility was not much more than 100 yards. He then came down to about 150 feet and cruised among the sand dunes trying to find landmarks like a road or a railway, but soon his fuel pump started playing up. He reckoned that if he did not do something about this soon, his engine would cut in about a quarter of an hour. So he headed back out to sea in case he was forced to land. There he saw a diving submarine. It can be presumed that he saw enough of the submarine to satisfy himself that it had no red and white marks on its conning tower, because he then dropped a bomb ahead of its track. The bomb did not explode. He now landed to try and sort out his engine. While Ross was attending to his engine, he noticed a trawler heading for him at full speed. He managed to swing his propeller, start his engine, clamber back into his cockpit and taxi off at speed into the haze, thereby escaping the attentions of the trawler. He then took off and headed for the rendezvous, where he saw the destroyers *Lurcher* and *Firedrake*. At about 0915 hrs, Ross landed and was taken in tow by *Lurcher*, with Keyes on board, which took him home to mother *Engadine* where he was hoisted on board at 1030.

All the other flights were variations on a theme similar to Ross's. All reported encountering fog over land, and especially over the target area. All reported sighting ships of various descriptions. Most of them were shot at and some of the planes were hit. Flight Sub Lieutenant Vivian Blackburn dropped two bombs on a gun battery that was giving him trouble, and a third on what he thought was the middle of Wilhelmshaven. There were no reported effects of any of the bombs. Flight Commander Douglas Oliver dropped all his bombs on what he thought might be a seaplane base on the island of Langeoog but was probably sheds or warehouses. Charles Edmonds had no more success finding the Zeppelin sheds but, in the face of heavy anti-aircraft fire, he bombed and missed the cruisers *Stralsund* and *Graudenz* in the Weser. He arrived safely back at the flotilla at 1020 with his plane damaged by shrapnel and bullet holes.

Cecil Kilner, with his observer Erskine Childers, submitted the most comprehensive and detailed report on the ships, lighthouses and other points of military interest that they had observed. Visibility was never much more than half a mile and they were compelled to fly at between 200 and 300 feet. Their difficulties were compounded by the engine which began to misfire. Having searched for the airship sheds and failed to find them in the fog, they realised that they might be forced to land, so they headed for the sea. The engine cheered up a bit as they emerged from the fog but they then came under heavy fire from anchored ships which damaged a float strut and severed rigging wires. Shortly afterwards, they were fired upon again from a wharf. Finally, having found no opportunity to bomb any target, and with the engine again spluttering unpleasantly, they turned for the rendezvous with the carriers which they reached successfully, five minutes before Edmonds.

Shortly after these three aircraft had been hoisted on board, the squadron came under attack again from two seaplanes. Once more there were near misses but no hits. British anti-aircraft fire was more effective this time and one of the aircraft was so badly holed that it was damaged beyond repair on landing back at Heligoland.

Malone had ordered that each aircraft should carry fuel sufficient for a three-hour flight. When ordering this, he would no doubt have taken into account the distance to target, the time required over target, and built in a contingency margin. He would also be conscious of the trade-off between fuel, bombs, passengers and the risk that, if too heavily laden, an aircraft might not be able to take off at all. In the event, three hours left no margin for error. However, in the same way that pilots could choose whether to have an observer or not, some of them apparently took the decision to take additional fuel. Perhaps it was at the suggestion of the captain of the *Riviera*, Flight Commander Robertson. In any event, *Riviera*'s aircraft appear to have had greater endurance than the others. Edmonds was in the air for three hours and ten minutes and arrived safely back at the carriers. Kilner and Childers did the same. But by 1030, with Ross having been retrieved by *Lurcher*, only three out of seven aircraft were accounted for.

A number of sweeps of the approaches north of the island of Norderney was made for lame ducks which might have just landed short of mother.

Nothing was found. With the number of Zeppelins and seaplanes that had encountered the British force, the Germans had had a fair idea what was facing them in the Heligoland Bight. However, their efforts were hampered by the fact that the radio of at least one of the Zeppelins was not working, and the seaplanes did not have radios. The German naval aviation arm had done its best with the limited resources at its disposal, and submarines were also deployed into the area to intercept the British on their way home. Three submarine attacks were mounted on the British during these final sweeps but the targets turned away unwittingly before torpedoes could be fired.[9]

Tyrwhitt was clearly deeply anxious for his missing pilots and planes. A concerned and engaged leader, the loss of four of his pilots and two observers, not to mention four scarce and precious aircraft, would matter keenly to him. But he also had the lives of many hundreds of other men in his hands. Four and a half hours after take-off time, he gave up and turned west for home, shadowed for part of the way by a Zeppelin. Tyrwhitt's only hope was that they might have survived to land at sea and been picked up by submarine. His hope was not misplaced.

A couple of hours earlier, Lieutenant Commander Martin Nasmith commanding submarine E11, which was submerged near Norderney Island, spotted a seaplane through his periscope. The red rings on the wings were visible even at 1,200 feet. He gave the order to surface. At almost precisely the same time the pilot, Flight Lieutenant Arnold Miley, in his Type 81, spotted Nasmith's periscope and, as the submarine rose, he observed the red and white markings on the conning tower. Having been fired at by several ships and gun batteries, and having cruised around hunting fruitlessly through the mist for anything worth bombing, he was now very low on fuel. To make sure of his location he came down and landed next to the submarine. On discovering that the fleet was 25 miles to the north, he prevailed upon Nasmith to give him a tow. As this unlikely combination was making its way northwards, a Zeppelin was spotted. At about the same time, two more seaplanes appeared. Both were British, both landed and both begged a lift from Nasmith. The first of these to land, with Vivian Blackburn and his observer James Bell, had a damaged float strut and it tipped its tail up in the air as it came alongside. Douglas Oliver and his observer Gilbert Budds landed close enough to step on board, but Blackburn and Bell had to swim for it from their sinking plane.

As if Nasmith's piece of ocean wasn't now crowded enough by friend and foe, another submarine was sighted. This one submerged before it could be positively identified, so Nasmith had to assume it was hostile. In fact it was another British submarine, D6, commanded by Lieutenant Commander Halahan, coming to assist E11. Halahan had submerged because he too feared an attack from the Zeppelin. In the face of aerial and possible sub-surface attack, there was no question of towing now, so all the aircraft were abandoned and Nasmith too gave the order to submerge. But before the submarine went down the crew managed to bring up a machine gun and riddle the aircraft floats.

Once below the surface, Nasmith turned his craft around to face the other submarine in order to present the smallest possible target. As the Zeppelin came overhead it dropped two bombs which shook both submarines but caused no damage. Nasmith, with five aviators aboard, recovered to Harwich in due course. Halahan, himself an aviator as well as a submariner, seeing at least one of the aircraft apparently intact, and not knowing that Nasmith had beat him to it, rose to rescue the pilot. The Zeppelin was still in the vicinity and sprayed D6 and the planes with machine-gun fire. Halahan submerged again, but not before he had satisfied himself that there were no stranded pilots and that the planes were all sinking.

This left one aircraft unaccounted for, a Type 135 flown by Flight Commander Francis Hewlett. Navigating under these circumstance must have been pretty uncertain, especially for pilots with no observer, and it is rather surprising that only one pilot got badly lost. Francis Hewlett, like everyone else, had taken off and had seen the Zeppelin by Heligoland Island. He had then entered the fog and had come down to 200 feet to try and get his bearings. He soon came across a large warship which saw him and opened fire at him. Shortly afterwards, he nearly collided with the masts and funnels of three or four further warships, which also opened fire on him. By now probably close to the target, he nevertheless failed to find the sheds in the fog and soon emerged into clear daylight above the open sea. With no ships, no land and no island to be seen, he headed south to make landfall again and try to orientate himself. He encountered a Zeppelin which fired at him but did not hit him. He knew that he could not outclimb the Zeppelin to bomb it, and that it more or less matched him in speed, he headed west to avoid it. Having shaken off the Zeppelin, he turned on to the bearing that he thought would take him to the rendezvous with the ships, however his oil pressure began to fall, and the engine began to overheat and misfire. He then saw a trawler flying the Dutch flag, so he glided down and landed next to her. The seaplane was secured to the trawler and he hopped on board. The problem with his engine was that it had run out of castor oil, but the Dutch trawler had none to give him. So he waited for the engine to cool in the hope that he might be able to make one more short journey to find the carriers – only to discover that the engine had seized and would not start. So the floats were punctured, and the plane was abandoned and sunk.

Having rescued him, the trawlermen still had a job to do and carried on fishing with their unexpected guest on board until they returned to their home port at Ymuiden seven days later. Hewlett was returned to the UK on 3 January 1915.

He was irked by the failure of his engine and felt responsible for it. In his report he explains at length that, on taking over the plane, he had noticed that the engine consumed a greater than normal quantity of oil, but that he had arranged with the mechanics to compensate for this. Somehow these arrangements had failed. He plainly felt partly let down, but also guilty, and deeply regretted that he 'should have caused so much trouble and should have necessitated the loss of a seaplane to the Naval Service'. One's heart goes out to him. That a man who has risked his life to fly over enemy territory under such parlous circumstances should feel guilty for the loss of his plane is a touching insight into the quality and commitment prevalent in the Royal Naval Air Service. There was much rejoicing and relief when it became known that he was safe and well.

Churchill ordered that the Cuxhaven pilots should select two of their number for the award of the Distinguished Service Order. They chose Kilner and Edmonds. Bell and Budds were given the Distinguished Service Medal, and a Mention in Dispatches went to Childers.

What was the outcome of the Cuxhaven Raid? Measured by success in achieving its stated objectives, it was a total failure. The British had no idea what damage they had inflicted, if any, although various rumours and estimates circulated. The official report has a note dated 27 January 1915 which talks about 'reliable' reports stating that extensive damage was done at Cuxhaven by the seaplane attack on Christmas Day.[10] It refers to a destroyer being struck and two colliers being sunk. It says that a revolving aircraft shed, a quay and some houses were damaged. Twelve civilians and 67 seamen were allegedly killed, and 36 civilians and 41 seamen wounded. The report mentions damage to coastal forts and gasworks. The British further believed that the raid had spooked the Germans into moving their ships in such a hurry that the battlecruiser *Von Der Tann* was severely damaged in a collision with another vessel. This was apparently confirmed by a statement made by some German sailors who had been rescued from SMS *Blücher* when she was sunk at the Battle of Dogger Bank in January 1915. This also alleged that the battlecruiser *Von Der Tann* had been seriously damaged. But this was all wishful thinking. Apart from the one seaplane mentioned above, there was no material damage of any kind – not counting the four seaplanes that the British themselves had lost. And unless one counts the four men washed overboard and lost from ships of the Grand Fleet many miles away in the North Sea, no one on either side lost their lives.

In his heart of hearts, Murray Sueter knew that his people had not achieved much of warlike significance. However, when his masters came to publish the official report, the central mission he had given the pilots – to destroy the Zeppelin sheds – had been conveniently forgotten. Instead, the subsidiary reconnaissance tasks had been elevated to the status of the main mission. The *London Gazette* states that 'an air reconnaissance of the Heligoland Bight, including Cuxhaven, Heligoland, and Wilhelmshaven was made by naval seaplanes, and the opportunity was taken at the same time of attacking with bombs points of Military Importance'[11]. This swapping of the mission with the secondary tasks was an elegant but barefaced instance of sexing up a report for public consumption.

No British pilot ever saw the target. Malone even wondered whether it existed at all. And yet, mysteriously, the target *was* the subject of an attack. At 0830 hrs on that Christmas Day a seaplane was seen approaching the Zeppelin hangar at Nordholz at 1,000 feet. The plane was fired at but showed no sign of being hit; it then dropped two bombs which fell in a wood nearby, and disappeared. Was it Oliver thinking it was a seaplane shed, or was it Blackburn trying to bomb a battery, or was it Ross or Miley trying to shed weight while struggling with a troublesome engine? One can only guess.

In any event, in a war where so much carnage was inflicted by both sides on each other, one can but marvel that so many ships, aircraft and submarines, all bent on inflicting death and destruction, achieved such a complete and singular failure. Furthermore, the information gathered so meticulously and at such risk by the pilots, and by the observers like Childers, Bell and Budds, was for the most part highly perishable and much of it was probably irrelevant within twenty-four hours. It was natural that the British should seek information on the German bases, but with a strategy of distant blockade in place, it was unlikely that much of it would ever be applied to any constructive or destructive purpose.

The German naval air arm and the subsurface fleet reacted quickly to these intruders in their back yard, but the surface element of the High Seas Fleet steadfastly refused to rise to the bait. Undoubtedly they were still smarting after the Battle of Heligoland Bight, and would continue to do so for some time to come. Nevertheless, their air arm was presumably able to tell the German command that there were no British surface heavies within striking distance. But the Germans would also know that such a force would not venture into the Bight without support of some sort, and if there were no supporting surface vessels, then there would undoubtedly be submarines. They probably smelt a rat. In this they would have been absolutely right, of course. They might also have decided that there was a distinct limit to the damage that this motley force of cruisers and destroyers, with their strange cross-Channel ferries, could inflict. This turned out to be correct under the circumstances, but the situation could easily have been quite different. Presumably, the German command judged it was not worth the risk of being lured into a trap. More prosaically, perhaps one should not rule out the simple possibility that it being Christmas Day might have militated against getting a fleet of powerful surface vessels to sea at very short notice.

The important thing was that the British did not *think* that the operation had been a complete waste of time. In spite of the apparent failure to achieve their stated aims, they felt the potential for great things had been demonstrated. The British were encouraged to continue to develop the concept and to try something similar again. They felt they had achieved a moral victory operating in Germany's back yard with relative impunity, although the German Naval Air Service could justifiably claim they had put up a respectable performance too. But whatever the reason for the absence of the High Seas Fleet, it helped to emphasise the British sense of moral victory.

However, moral victories don't win wars. Of much greater importance was what was learned about operating aircraft in hostile waters. Some lessons were applied quickly within a few months, and some took a little longer. At the end of his report, Cecil Malone of the *Engadine* mused: 'I look upon the events which took place on 25 December as visible proof of the probable line in the development of the principles of naval strategy.' He went on to say: 'One can well imagine what might have been done had our seaplanes, or those which were sent out to attack us, carried torpedoes or light guns.' Prophetic words indeed, especially for one so junior. His masters plainly had similar thoughts. The successor to the Type 136 seaplane was designed from inception as a torpedo-bomber. Was there, intertwined with thankfulness for deliverance, a certain gleam in his eye? Possibly, because the following year in the Dardanelles, Charles Edmonds, flying from HMS *Ben-my-Chree*, commanded by Cecil Malone, would carry out the first ever successful air-delivered torpedo attack on a ship.

The Cuxhaven Raid added impetus and helped to justify a number of initiatives which were already under way. In this way, it played an important part in the evolution of the aircraft carrier as an instrument of offence and defence. It was also a portent of the future in that it was the first sea battle where airborne craft were the sole means whereby the enemy was engaged, on both sides.

The capability of *Engadine*, *Empress* and *Riviera* was soon improved by replacing the canvas hangars with bespoke steel hangars. The Isle of Man ferry, *Ben-my-Chree*, taken in hand for conversion to a seaplane carrier at the beginning of 1915, was given the same capability. *Ark Royal*, with her pioneering internal aircraft hangar, had already been commissioned in early December 1914.

But the British knew they had been lucky on the Cuxhaven Raid. The lesson of that fraught, helpless, vulnerable moment when the ships had stopped to hoist out the seaplanes was not lost on them. They knew they had to develop a means of launching aircraft without exposing their ships unduly to the attentions of an enemy. The moment of aircraft recovery was, if anything, even more important, because any protection that might have been offered by surprise in the take-off phase would surely have been lost by the time of recovery. So they needed to develop a ship which could launch and recover aircraft without disrupting the normal warlike operations of the fleet. This meant launching and retrieving while the ship was underway, rather than hoisting out on to, and in from the water. The liner *Campania* had already been purchased in November 1914, and she was in the process of being converted with a launch deck forward so that larger seaplanes on trolleys could take off from her. This service she performed for the Grand Fleet based at Scapa Flow from the summer of 1915. However, her ramp was felt to be too short and she went back into refit to have it extended. Not until April 1916 was she capable of launching aircraft reliably while underway. *Ben-my-Chree* was also completed with a flying-off deck, as were the other two ferries converted in 1915, *Vindex* and *Manxman*. Another lesson from the Cuxhaven Raid was how dependent seaplane operations were on good weather. The weather at sea on 25 December had been excellent and operations had gone ahead unimpeded. But the previous attempt in October 1914 had been abandoned because it would have been impossible to launch in bad weather. Seaplanes were used throughout the war, but from 1914 onwards, the trend towards the use of ship-launched aircraft – first on trolleys and skids, then on wheels – became more and more marked.

Perversely, some of the urgency was dissipated when the Zeppelins conducted their first bombing raid over England in January 1915. The British had consistently overestimated the number of airships available to Germany, and the destructive effect they might have. When the grand total of two airships raided in January, killing four people and damaging a few houses and a power station, it was something of an anti-climax. This wasn't quite how H.G. Wells said it would be. The fear of the unknown, now it was known, lost some of its power to terrify. Although the raids were to continue through to July 1918, and they never lost their 'bogey' aura, people soon began to understand that they caused more alarm than damage.

In parallel with this, enemy submarines soon became a more pressing preoccupation than Zeppelins. The efforts to counter their real and present underwater threat, and to keep the British Isles supplied with the necessary materials to live and to fight, eclipsed the need to protect against an air threat which, however devastating in theory, had yet to live up to its promise.

Furthermore, Churchill's departure from the Admiralty in May 1915, as a result of failure in the Dardanelles, subtracted somewhat from the focus that he had supplied to the destruction of Zeppelins. The commitment of resources to the Dardanelles theatre also constrained efforts in the North Sea.

Nevertheless, throughout the war, Zeppelins never ceased to be a cause for concern for the Royal Navy, and the requirement to extend the range of aircraft in order to hit their bases played a part in carrier development right up to the end. The Zeppelins' ability to spy on the Grand Fleet, although the Germans didn't use it to the full and British anti-aircraft capability steadily improved, gave them an edge which they never entirely lost. The possibility that they might add exponential potency to the German submarine campaign was also an ever-present spectre. Up until February 1916, the Royal Navy was responsible for defending Britain against Zeppelin attacks. At that point, this responsibility, which had lain with the Army until the beginning of the war, was handed back to the Army. Even so, Commodore Tyrwhitt continued to hatch plans to conduct a repeat of the Cuxhaven operation.

Ships and submarines deployed again on 23 January 1915, but that operation was forestalled by the Battle of Dogger Bank on 24 January. Another attempt was made on 29 January but the weather was foul and the ships returned to base without having attempted an aircraft launch. Although Cuxhaven was not attacked again, on 20 March a similar operation was mounted on the German radio station at Norddeich. Weather again prevented take-off and three days later, fog on the enemy coast stymied another attempt. Once more, on 3 May, weather made seaplane launching impossible, and yet again fog foiled them three days after that.

Tyrwhitt was nothing if not persistent and, on 11 May, the Harwich Force managed to launch three seaplanes. One crashed on landing. The plane was wrecked but the pilot was saved. Another crashed into the sea and was never seen again. Only the third returned safely.

Almost all of these operations would have had a better chance of success if it had been possible to launch a plane directly from a ship. On the last of these attempts, the newly converted *Ben-my-Chree* actually tried to launch a Sopwith Schneider seaplane from its flying-off deck but the aircraft engine failed.

For the remainder of 1915 and 1916, there was a litany of attempted raids which were abandoned through bad weather or technical failure of engines or aeroplanes. Even after the *Vindex* joined Harwich Force with her forward launch deck, they were unlucky. In March 1916, she launched five seaplanes, but three suffered engine failure and the pilots were captured. For some officers like Jellicoe, who was having a similar experience at Scapa Flow with *Campania*, this catalogue of failure undermined their faith in seaplanes and the Royal Naval Air Service. Others like Tyrwhitt knew they were simply relearning the lessons of the Cuxhaven Raid and that if they could get the right combination of ship and aircraft, the weather would be a less dominant factor and fortune would surely be more inclined to smile upon them. They knew that what they required was a true through-deck aircraft carrier which would be able to launch and recover aircraft more independently of the sea state, and they continued to press for such a ship. But the demand on the shipyards to build other types of warships was heavy and the new concept had to take its turn.

Meanwhile merchant ships continued to be converted with forward launch decks but with no means of shipboard recovery. *Pegasus* and *Nariana*[12] were bought while under construction and were commissioned in 1917 to operate seaplanes aft, and land planes forward. The battlecruiser *Furious* was also converted during construction and, instead of a forward 18-inch gun, she too was given a forward aircraft launch ramp. But a forward launch deck only solved half the problem. Work continued to equip the fleet with aircraft that could land on as well as take off from a ship underway. One brave pilot, Squadron Commander Edwin Dunning, succeeded in landing on *Furious* by approaching from the stern and side-slipping onto the forward deck after dodging the funnel and the superstructure. He tried it once too often and was killed on the third attempt. *Furious* was soon given a landing-on deck aft of the funnel but that, too, proved a dangerous proposition, much interfered with by the exhaust fumes and the air turbulence generated by the superstructure. The cruiser *Vindictive* was similarly equipped and wasn't any more successful.

Both the potential and the limitations of this halfway house, or 'mixed carrier' concept, could not have been more starkly illustrated by the air raid that took place on the Tondern Zeppelin base on the Schleswig Holstein coast on 19 July 1918. Early in the morning, HMS *Furious* launched seven Sopwith Camels, each carrying two 50lb bombs. The Sopwith Camel was a wheeled aircraft and one of the finest machines to be produced during the war on either side. One aircraft did not make it as far as the coast; it crashed in the sea and the pilot was drowned. But the other six pressed on and carried out the most successful carrier operation of the war. The Tondern sheds were hit and the two modern Zeppelins inside them totally destroyed. But that was where the success ended. The unsatisfactory design of *Furious* meant that she could not recover her aircraft. Four aircraft were forced by bad weather to land in Denmark. The remaining two did get back to the ship but were unable to land on and were forced to ditch in the sea, although the pilots survived.[13] One cannot help surmising that even if any of the other five aircraft had made it back to the ship, they would almost certainly have shared the same fate. Thereafter, *Furious* was relegated to kite balloon service until the end of the war. She was finally converted to a full through-deck carrier after hostilities were over.

The Cuxhaven raid had been an attempt to destroy Zeppelins on land because, at that time, they could not be destroyed in the air. However, the performance of heavier-than-air aircraft was steadily improving and by 1917 there were some, like the Sopwith Camel, coming into service that had a chance of reaching Zeppelins and shooting them down. However, none of these types were seaplanes. Later seaplanes did bring down Zeppelins but, while the seaplane had utility as a reconnaissance aircraft, and even as an attacker of ship and ground targets, it was less likely to be an aerial match for an airship that carried half a dozen machine guns and could ascend speedily and routinely to 15,000 feet or more. Thus, notwithstanding the appearance of more and better anti-aircraft guns, the Royal Navy still remained largely impotent in the face of scouting Zeppelins. In July 1915, Admiral Jellicoe spelt out this weakness to the Admiralty. He pointed out that air spotting would unquestionably be used to great advantage by the Germans. We shall be 'unable to prevent the Germans by doing so by means of their Zeppelins'.[14] So the momentum to acquire a true onboard launch-and-recovery capability of modern wheeled aircraft was now given a double push by the Zeppelin threat.

At last, in September 1916, the Admiralty gave instructions to build a true through-deck carrier. She too was a liner which had been taken in hand during construction. Her charthouse and bridge were raised and lowered on a hydraulic lift as required, and her masts and flag-jacks all folded down flat. The engine exhausts were funnelled out sideways and expelled by fans over the stern so she had an unobstructed, level flying deck 550 feet long and 68 feet wide. She had two lifts for raising and lowering aircraft between the flight deck and her 350-foot-long internal hangar. With a speed of 20 knots, she was thus purpose built to fly and maintain aircraft, and operate in conjunction with the Fleet. Launched in December 1917, and completed in September 1918, HMS *Argus* came into service too late to see action in the First World War. Between the wars she was used chiefly in an experimental and training role, but she briefly saw active service as a combat carrier in the Mediterranean in the Second World

War. *Argus* has bequeathed her concept and function to every combat aircraft carrier since.

So the Zeppelin played an important part in the evolution of the aircraft carrier in two ways: the need to extend the range of aircraft so that they could strike the Zeppelin sheds helped to develop the strike carrier role; and the fear of unwanted observation by Zeppelins fostered the fleet defence role. Both these roles were to continue in one form or another – and continue today – long after the Zeppelins have disappeared from the skies. The aircraft carrier of today can trace its pedigree to the extraordinary lighter-than-air machine created by an elderly, distinguished officer of the German Army, and the long-gone floating shed he built for it by the shores of Lake Constance.

Ultimately Winston Churchill was right. It was the aircraft that did for them in the end. But in 1914, the aircraft was an uncertain, untried offensive weapon. Charles Collet, Reggie Marix, Eugene Gerrard, Spenser Grey, John Babington, Sidney Sippe, Edward Briggs, Robert Ross, Arnold Miley, Francis Hewlett, Charles Edmonds, Vivian Blackburn with James Bell, Douglas Oliver with Gilbert Budds, and Cecil Kilner with Erskine Childers were the first men to try it. Their legacy is with us still.

Let their epitaph be written by Churchill, who inspired and guided the effort on the British side. He said that, at the beginning of the war:

> Our resources were feeble and slender. Compared to the developments at the end of the war they were puny. Still, they were all we had, and all that our knowledge of aviation at that time could bestow. Deficiencies in material had to be made good by daring …
> All honour to the naval airmen, the pioneers of the aerial offensive, who planned and executed in these early months the desperate flights over hostile territory in an element then scarcely known, which resulted in the raids on Düsseldorf and Cologne on the Rhine, Friedrichshafen on Lake Constance, and Cuxhaven in the Heligoland Bight. Altogether in the first twelve months of the war six Zeppelins were destroyed in the air or in their sheds by the offensive action of a handful of British airmen.[15]

All honour indeed.

Notes

1 Royal Naval Air Service Operational Reports ADM 116/1352 at Public Record Office, Kew.

2 Ibid.

3 Ibid.

4 Ibid.

5 Layman, R.D., *The Cuxhaven Raid: The World's First Carrier Air Strike*, Conway Maritime Press, 1985, p. 61.

6 The aircraft was a Gotha Taube. The Taube was a monoplane of singular ethereal elegance. It had no tail rudder, and had wings and tail which made it look like a flying dove, hence the name *taube*, meaning 'dove' in German. In spite of its name, its shape was in fact inspired by the *Zanonia macrocarpa* seeds which have a single wing not unlike a sycamore 'helicopter' seed. The wings were translucent and made it difficult to spot at height, thus it is sometimes referred to as the world's first 'stealth' plane.

7 Layman, *The Cuxhaven*Raid, p. 66.

8 Robinson, Douglas, *The Zeppelin in Combat*,Foulis & Co., 1971, p. 46.

9 Layman, *The Cuxhaven Raid*, p. 109.

10 Royal Naval Air Service Operational Reports ADM 116/1352 at Public Record Office, Kew.

11 1721 Supplement to the *London Gazette*, 19 February 1915.

12 Most sources spell the name of this ship 'Nairana' but I have taken the spelling in *Jane's Fighting Ships of World War I* as authoritative.

13 Robinson, Douglas, *The Zeppelin in Combat*,Foulis & Co., 1971, p. 318.

14 Jones, H.A., *Official History of the War: The War in the Air*,vol II, OUP, 1928, p. 364.

15 Churchill, Winston, *The World Crisis 1911-1914*. p. 314.

Chapter 6

The 'Menace'

For more than a year of war, the Zeppelin gave Germany the potential for strategic supremacy in the air. It was the fear of this domination of the new dimension of war which had spurred the British, first into trying to match it, and, when the *Mayfly* broke its back, into finding other means of countering it. Although the Royal Flying Corps is best remembered now for its support of the land war on the Western Front, it was the airship threat which dominated the minds of those who ordered its creation. The Royal Flying Corps was a child of the Zeppelin, even if that Corps quickly chose to ignore its parentage.

But the nightmares of the British never came to pass. The Royal Navy was not seriously constrained in its use of the North Sea by the enemy's air reconnaissance. The German High Seas Fleet did not use the intelligence that the Zeppelin might have supplied to it to bring the British to battle on terms of its choosing. Neither did the Zeppelin bring devastation and destruction to the heart of Empire such that the British people would force their leaders to sue for terms. It didn't come anywhere near it. So how did the Germans use the Zeppelin, and why was it not used to better effect?

It is doubtful whether the Imperial German Navy really understood the potential of the weapons they had in their hands until it was too late. Grand Admiral Alfred von Tirpitz had concentrated on building the Navy for its political effect, but had given less thought to how it might be employed operationally. He was not an aviation enthusiast and seemed indifferent to the advantages Zeppelins conferred on the German Navy, advantages which seemed all too obvious to his enemies. Only in 1914 did he give the Zeppelin project any real support. In reality, while the Imperial German Navy may have been technically superior in some ways to the Royal Navy, it too suffered from poor strategic leadership, ill-thought-out war plans, sketchy concepts of operations and a less-than-satisfactory command structure.

To begin with, the Germans were convinced that the British would attempt a close blockade of Germany – the traditional blockade that the British had placed on the French over a hundred years earlier. The Germans were confident that their mines and formidable torpedo forces would be a powerful counter to this close blockade and would inflict grave damage. But Admiral John Jellicoe commanding the British fleet was a prudent and cautious commander. As Churchill said, 'he was the only man on either side who could lose the war in an afternoon', and he was not therefore going to expose his crown jewels to this obvious lethal threat. With his ships conducting a distant blockade, operating out of their bases in Rosyth and the Northern Isles, the Germans realized they needed more Zeppelins to conduct patrols in these farther waters and so started an intensive building programme. They also resorted to the idea that, rather than confront the entire British fleet, they might destroy isolated detachments of it piecemeal and thereby reduce its numerical superiority.

For this strategy, the Zeppelin was an ideal scout. But even this approach faded into a faint wish after the Battle of Heligoland on 28 August 1914. During this battle, British battlecruisers had destroyed three German cruisers which had been conducting regular patrols near that island. The British had garnered the relevant intelligence by deploying submarines into the operational area. The only Zeppelin that the German Navy possessed at that time was deployed too late and returned to base after being fired at by its own ships. Had it done what it was told to do, it might have spotted the British heavy units and prevented the loss of the three German cruisers. The chief lesson that was there for the learning was that, if more Zeppelins had been deployed in the right areas, not only might they have prevented this catastrophe, but the Germans might even have been able to surprise the British with their own heavies. Instead, the German heavy units remained swinging at anchor off their base at Wilhelmshaven. The Germans were greatly discouraged by the Heligoland battle from thereafter venturing out at all.

But venture out again they did and at the Battle of Dogger Bank on 23 January the following year, an airship was present at a naval battle for the first and last time in history. However, the German Navy had still not worked out a proper doctrine for their use in battle and continued to use them defensively. Instead of seeking out British units that might be ambushed, they used Zeppelins to report on the absence of British units. German battlecruisers were pursued by British battlecruisers and one of them, the *Blücher*, was destroyed. But earlier in the action, one of the British ships had been damaged and was detached and so was highly vulnerable. However, the Zeppelin confined itself to tracking German ships instead of keeping tabs on the British ones, and the opportunity to destroy a major British unit was missed.

Admiral Reinhard Scheer, the commander of the German High Seas Fleet, had intended to use his Zeppelins at the Battle of Jutland on 31 May 1916 to avoid being surprised and brought to battle against his will. It is clear that he had hoped to use them in a much more adventurous sweep rather than simply confining them to close-in tactical reconnaissance. However, the weather was unfavourable and he went ahead without them. Ten Zeppelins did eventually take off before the battle was over in the hope that they might be of some assistance. They weren't, playing no part in the daytime battle of 31 May 1916. Two of them witnessed the confused melée of the night battle but took no active part in it. If a realistic doctrine had been worked out and practised, Scheer might have planned his operation taking into account the weather and ensuring that he would be able to make use of this platform which gave him a clear edge over the British.

Jutland was a battle of surprises. The British knew that the Germans were at sea because of radio intercepts, and so Beatty, commanding the British battlecruisers, was able to surprise Admiral Franz von Hipper, commanding the German battlecruisers. In pursuing them, Beatty, instead of destroying his quarry, was to his own surprise outgunned by Hipper and lost two of his own battlecruisers. Some of the surprises for the British were self-inflicted because the radio intercepts, which should have given them a battle-winning advantage, had been passed on inefficiently and incompletely. Beatty was thus surprised by the appearance of Scheer commanding the German battleships. Beatty turned to run and in doing so nearly lost the new battleship *Warspite*. In chasing Beatty, Scheer in turn was surprised by the appearance of Jellicoe commanding the British battleships, and only escaped a grave mauling by a narrow margin. So, tactically, the battle was inconclusive. War is the province of the unexpected, but if the Germans had been able to use their Zeppelins more aggressively, they would have increased their chances of ensuring that the most unpleasant surprises rested with Beatty and Jellicoe.

But Scheer was not the only admiral who did not take full advantage of the opportunities that naval aviation offered at Jutland. The seaplane carrier HMS *Campania* had rejoined the Grand Fleet at Scapa Flow after a refit which extended her forward launching deck from 120 feet to 200 feet. This made her a more capable launching platform and made her less dependent on good weather. She received the preparatory order to sail with the Grand Fleet for the Jutland battle, but somehow the executive order did not reach her. *Campania*'s berth was out of line of sight of the main anchorage and no one noticed that she had not accompanied the Fleet until over two hours later. She eventually sailed and struggled to catch up but, when Jellicoe heard of her situation, he feared that, on her own, she would be an easy target for submarines and dismissed her back to Scapa on the morning of 31 May.

Jellicoe was conscious of the value of maritime air, but his experience with *Campania* before her refit had been that she was more trouble than she was worth. Presumably he assumed that he had plenty of cruisers and battlecruisers to seek out the High Seas Fleet for him. However Beatty, while performing his purpose admirably in delivering his pursuers, the German High Seas Fleet, to the guns of Jellicoe, failed conspicuously to tell Jellicoe what was happening. Had Jellicoe, on the evening of 31 May, been better informed of the locations and dispositions of the ships that were about to be lured into his trap, he might have been better prepared for this fleeting encounter of the two most powerful navies in the world. What Jellicoe really needed at Jutland was information. What might have happened if *Campania*'s capable Type 184 seaplanes had been able to fill the gaps in Beatty's reports is another intriguing 'what if' of history.

The action involving Beatty's Battlecruiser Fleet offers another glimpse of what might have happened. Beatty too needed information and he had the seaplane carrier *Engadine* under command. She had two Short 184s embarked. One of these took off, accurately identified Hipper's advance cruisers and destroyers, and passed the message back to the carrier. Given the poor weather and the friction of war, this was no mean achievement. However, as a result of the afflictions of Murphy's Law which attend all military operations, the message was not passed on, and the aircraft suffered mechanical difficulties. No other flights were ordered or attempted in the increasingly marginal weather. The aircraft did not affect the course of the battle, but if there had been more than one seaplane carrier, or if Mars had rolled his dice differently, then the fog of war might have dispersed more readily in front of Beatty.

Admiral Scheer made another attempt at cutting out isolated British units later that summer on 18 August 1916. This time he did deploy his airships. But he deployed them too late, and the British had already passed the line of their patrols by the time they arrived on station. The British also sensed that Scheer was up to something because of the unusual Zeppelin activity in the North Sea and were able to act accordingly. Had Zeppelin activity been more routinely seen in the North Sea, their suspicions may not have been aroused.

Scheer undoubtedly learned as the war progressed but by the time he got round to using Zeppelins more closely to their full potential, it was too late. During 1914 and 1915, the Zeppelin offered a naval scouting capability to which the British had no effective answer, and the British knew it. That was, after all, why the Royal Naval Air Service was set to bombing them in their sheds. But by late 1916 the British anti-aircraft capability had developed to the point that it was unsafe to be seen within range of British ships. British seaplanes were becoming more and more capable and the Zeppelin's edge had been blunted. Even then, the British were always wary of them. Seaplanes were not the best match in the air for a craft that could rise so fast and so high. The British were also ever conscious that, in spite of the advantage which their own radio intercept capability gave them, the Germans might one day pull a trick with their Zeppelins and inflict catastrophic surprise on them, bringing them to battle at a time and place of the Germans' choosing. In such circumstances, the British overall superiority in numbers would count for nought.

More critically, the Zeppelin's potential for supporting what became unrestricted submarine warfare was barely touched. Had they carried fuel instead of the ordnance and ballast necessary for bombing raids, the later machines would have had a range of 3,000 miles and could have stayed aloft for several days. What they might have achieved out in the Atlantic, spotting merchant shipping and guiding submarines to their targets, will never be known. The submarine was the weapon that nearly brought Britain to her knees. Submarines supported by Zeppelins scouting for targets, even with all the limitations the weather might have placed upon them, could only have been even more effective. This must surely be yet another of the more tantalising 'what ifs' in history. Supporting the Fleet in this way should have been the Zeppelins' principle task. Instead, their efforts were dissipated on what ultimately turned out to be a futile strategic bombing campaign.

The German Army had no clearer ideas about how best to use their Zeppelins than the Navy. In the first month of the war, they cast them away on tactical bombing and reconnaissance operations with breathtaking profligacy. In early August 1914, the German Army lost their first craft while bombing forts near Liège at low altitude. Riddled by ground fire, so much gas leaked out that it crashed before it could make it back to base. The following day a second Zeppelin was lost while conducting a reconnaissance at 3,000 feet in the Vosges. Again it was riddled with bullets by ground troops. The same day some German troops near Trier applied the 'shoot first, ask questions later' principle and peppered another of their own Zeppelins outward bound from that town. The airship then found itself over French trenches at a height of only a few hundred feet. One can only guess at who was more surprised: the crew of the Zeppelin, or the French troops who found themselves presented with a target 520 feet wide at close range. They didn't miss, but the airship did not burst into flames – instead it staggered off to crash elsewhere. So in forty-eight hours, the German Army had lost three quarters of its serviceable dirigible airships. The fourth serviceable ship meanwhile dropped artillery shells on Liège, most of which did not explode, and two weeks later it bombed Antwerp. This was the machine that Reginald Marix destroyed when he bombed the shed at Düsseldorf on 8 October 1914. By then, the German Army had taken over a number of commercial machines and these, together with the new ones that they subsequently acquired, joined the naval types in their bombing missions over Britain. The German Army was less seized with the virtues of strategic bombing than the Navy, but they played their part in attacking Britain as much out of inter-service rivalry as anything.

The cost in resources that the British had to deploy to counter the Zeppelins was of course substantial, and these were men and materials that could not be sent to France. Furthermore, there were unseen costs with each raid. Loss and disruption of industrial production, snarled up railway timetables, increased absenteeism, and the general friction associated with living and working in the blackout – all these must be put into the balance when assessing the effect of the raids. The cost in broken bodies and shattered lives cannot objectively be counted, but a total of 557 people were killed by Zeppelin raids in the First World War. If one takes the total number of British Empire dead sustained over the 1,560 days of war as 908,000, then the daily average of dead was 582 souls. The comparison speaks for itself.

The cost of damage inflicted was estimated at £1.5 million – a substantial figure no doubt but equivalent to only half the cost of building one *Queen Elizabeth* class battleship. A further comparison may be made with the damage caused by accidental explosions in munitions factories during the war. The greatest of these, at Silvertown in East London in January 1917, is estimated to have caused more damage than all the air raids on the capital put together.[1]

To begin with, the effect of the Zeppelin raids on the morale of British civilians was considerable. But this fear was a fear of the unknown. When, after the first few raids, it became clear that they were not all going to be fried in their beds, British hysteria subsided and most people turned their attention to more pressing concerns. By September 1916, *Punch* felt able to lampoon Graf Zeppelin in a cartoon showing him in his office, perched on top of his stool at his drawing board, dreaming up ever more fantastic airborne contraptions. The Kaiser has startled him and is poking him in the chest. 'Tell me, Count, why didn't you invent something useful, like the tank?'

In these terms, the losses inflicted were trifling and certainly a long, long way from shattering the vital nerve centres and breaking the will of the people to continue the war.

The German authorities were seduced by their own propaganda. Like the British in the next war, they became fixated with the idea that they could bomb their adversary into submission, and by far the greater portion of their Zeppelin effort went into trying to achieve this. This notion was no doubt encouraged by inter-service rivalry – to which Service will victory be accredited? Neither Service wanted the other to have all the action and so they wound each other up. But after the first few raids, the British authorities, while recognising that they had to protect their people, no longer feared the Zeppelin as the ultimate bombing weapon. As strategic bombers, Zeppelins were an abject failure and the material effect they had was largely irrelevant.

Admiral Scheer only ever had a maximum of eighteen Zeppelins at his disposal. If he had fully understood their potential earlier, he might have pressed for more, and the efforts of the ones he had might have been more fruitfully directed. Airships of course had major limitations. Flying over the North Sea was never straightforward. Sudden squalls, mists, adverse headwinds, storms, rain, ice, snow, low cloud and the dreaded thunderstorms are part of normal daily life there, and, unlike a ship, the Zeppelin could not stay on task for more than a few hours at a time. Nevertheless, doctrine, tactics and training, if they had been developed from the experience gained, could have gone a long way to mitigating their shortcomings and using their potential to the full. But there was no will to do so.

So, rather than fulfilling the fears of their enemies, the Germans did not use their priceless advantage in the air to neutralise the superior numbers of the British Fleet. Instead, deluded by H.G. Wells, tantalised by Giulio Douhet, the great prophet of airpower, and seduced by their own propaganda, they dissipated it on a grand, vainglorious and futile attempt to knock Britain out of the fight by destroying her ability to wage war, and shattering the will of her people to continue the struggle.

To set out to study any aspect of the First World War – known as the 'Great War' until an even greater one overwhelmed the world twenty years later – is not to embark on a journey of joy. It is difficult to avoid a feeling of sadness at the folly which allowed mankind to be drawn into a conflagration that ripped the guts out of the European continent, and a few other parts of the world besides, and brought about the end of the historical European lead in world affairs. Indeed, peering back through a 21st-century lens, the war between Britain, Germany and France looks increasingly like a civil war – a war between brothers and sisters. And civil wars have often turned out to be the worst of all wars. One can argue with some justification that the peaceful Europe of today might never have come about if it had not had to endure the purge of war to resolve centuries of enmity. But at what a terrible cost. Was there no other way in the years between 1890 and 1914 to bring people to their senses?

But these are the musings of luxury. They are the conclusions of that most exact of sciences: hindsight. We too easily forget that Germany, Britain and France were fiercely independent countries, each with competing world empires. France was hurting for revenge against Germany after her humiliating defeat in 1871. England and France had been mortal enemies for centuries and only relatively recently had they found an accommodation in the face of a common threat. The surprise for our forefathers was not so much that they found themselves at war, but that Germany and Britain were on opposing sides; and that France and Britain were fighting together alongside another long-standing enemy, Russia.

Once war was engaged, it was plain that it had to be fought to the end with utmost resolution. So, while one is unavoidably touched with a sense of sadness, even nearly a hundred years later, one is also struck by the characters and the outstanding qualities of the men and women who fought it on all sides. Nowhere were these remarkable characters more in evidence than in the air. The gallantry required to go up in a rickety, IKEA-style, flatpack biplane constructed from plywood, piano wire and varnished linen or cotton, with an uncertain engine, and fly by day and night in all weathers over land and sea, is prodigious. Often without a radio, certainly without a parachute and usually in the face of a lethal enemy, these people demonstrated extraordinary gallantry and fortitude by any measure.

To ascend to 10,000 feet suspended under two million cubic feet of highly flammable gas again and again, and set off for many hundreds of miles across the sea at night into unknown enemy territory, also without a parachute, not knowing how the weather might change before you turned for home again – one is found wanting for words to describe the courage and resolution this must have demanded.

From the ground, the Zeppelins looked such calm, serene creations. The size of a battleship or an ocean liner, they imparted a sense of sinister, overwhelming power. Indeed many people, including Captain Murray Sueter, referred to them as 'dreadnought airships'. For Londoners, it must have been a terrifying experience to see Zeppelins above them in the sky at night, apparently inviolate, and able to strike at the heart of their empire at leisure. But when one reads the accounts of the difficulties that airship aviators faced, one learns a very different story. For a start, more often than not, they seem to have been uncertain of where they were. At night, often in cloud, flying over a blacked-out country, with a sextant, a watch, and a map and compass, navigation was not a precise science. Gross navigational errors were common. One raider reported he was bombing the naval installation at Rosyth on the River Forth. In fact he had been seduced by the estuary of the River Tay and his bombs were dropping 60 miles away in a field near Arbroath. He was by no means unusual in his outrageous lack of accuracy. Radio direction finding was introduced, but this required the Zeppelin to transmit radio signals to a station on the German coast. The German station then responded with a bearing of the Zeppelin. To get another bearing, the airship had to repeat the process with another station, and so on. The British of course listened to these transmissions and could do their sums too, and from time to time they jammed the transmissions. Anti-aircraft measures steadily improved as the war went on and before the war's end, aircraft were bringing Zeppelins down again and again. Only once during the war was an aircraft beaten by a Zeppelin in an air-to-air shootout.

The German answer was to fly higher and higher until they were routinely operating at 20,000 feet. In the sense that they were exploring a world where no man had been before, they can be compared to the early astronauts in our own era. One machine actually reached 24,000 feet. This took them beyond the range of all ground-based anti-aircraft defences, and above the ceiling of almost all aircraft, but brought a new sheaf of problems. They needed oxygen, for a start, and this was supplied, but it took a lot of men some persuading to use it. The temperature at such heights is routinely minus 40° Celsius so they also suffered bitter cold and frostbite. The gondolas were enclosed by now but were unheated, and men still had to man the machine-gun posts on top and at the rear of the craft. Aviation medicine was largely unknown, and the effects on the body of working for prolonged periods at such altitudes, the strain on the heart and lungs, nausea, dizziness, ringing in the ears, reduced efficiency and exhaustion – all these had to be learned about the hard way. The adverse effect of altitude on the machinery was also discovered. Engines became less efficient, radiator water evaporated more quickly and machinery iced up. Ballast water froze and the anti-freeze they used was corrosive. They discovered that the weather was also different at great height and they did not have the means to forecast it. Navigation was more complex and bombing accuracy was made even more difficult than it routinely was. This was not helped by compasses which froze. So while Zeppelins were safer from the British at these great heights, the threat they presented was nullified and they had to continue to come down and expose themselves at lower levels to have any operational military effect at all.

Bombing accuracy was never very good. They had a primitive bomb sight, but like the British, it was a problem they never solved properly. Again and again one reads of bombs being dropped miles from where the aviators thought they were. At one stage, so many bombs were dropped in open fields that the British thought the Germans were trying to destroy their crops. But the aviators convinced themselves that they were inflicting untold damage on factories, coal mines, warehouses and other vital infrastructure, the loss of which would surely bring the war to a favourable conclusion soon.

Zeppelins usually only deployed on moonless nights and, to a great degree, were always at the mercy of the weather. A description of a Zeppelin in a thunderstorm over the North Sea gives a flavour.

The Zeppelin was tossed violently up and down in the black boiling clouds, sometimes to within a thousand feet of the water. Rain lashed down in torrents. Blinding flashes of lightning surrounded the ship, leaping from cloud to cloud and from cloud to sea, and everything was heavily charged with electricity ... bluish-violet tongues of St Elmo's Fire a foot long burned on the machine gun sights, and the lookouts' heads were haloed in flame attracted by the wire in their caps. In the control car, the commander observed the same cold bluish flame spraying from his fingers when he held them out the window. Acutely aware that he was nearly a mile up in the air in a vessel supported by a million cubic feet of hydrogen, the commander was worried.[2]

He knew that if any of the gas escaped through the pressure valves, the ship would burn in the air.

That airship was lucky. On another occasion, the ground crew, who were waiting for a Zeppelin coming in from a raid, saw in the direction from which the airship was expected 'a large flash of flame like that of an explosion, which left a large cloud of smoke'. Others closer saw 'a flash of lightning, then a red flame burst out of the hull between the nose and the forward gondola. The fire climbed up the envelope, then the bows of the airship canted downwards to an angle of 80 degrees, and she slowly fell smothered in flame'.[3] None of her crew survived. One man who did survive such a conflagration on another occasion, Machinist's Mate Heinrich Ellerkam, has left us this glimpse of Hell with his account. His Zeppelin, L48, was attacked by British aircraft 11,000 feet over Holly Tree Farm, at Theberton in Suffolk.

There was a burst of gunfire and I could actually see phosphorous bullets tearing through the after cells ... I knew this must be the end ... there was an explosion – not loud, but a dull 'woof' as when you light a gas stove. A burst of flame, then another explosion. One gas cell after another was catching fire over my head. My first thought was not to be crushed under the wreckage in case we were over land, so I climbed further up among the girders. Flames were dancing everywhere and the heat was overpowering. My fur coat collar caught fire; I tried to beat it out with my hands ... the ship tipped vertically and down we plunged, a monstrous roaring banner of flame reaching hundreds of metres above my head, and the wind whistling through the bared framework. I noticed the draught was driving the flames away from me. But it was only a temporary respite. I thought of jumping ... We did not carry poison or pistols to shoot ourselves when the ship caught fire. Hand guns were forbidden. I was still arguing with myself when a light appeared below – whether on land or on sea, I could not tell. Suddenly there was a continuing roaring and smashing of metal as the stern struck the ground and the hull structure collapsed beneath me. I found myself on the ground with the breath half knocked out of me, the framework crashing down on top of me, fuel and oil tanks bursting on impact and their burning contents flowing towards me through the shattered wreckage. I was trapped in a tangle of red hot girders, the heat roasting me alive through my heavy flying coat. If I had lost consciousness, I would have burned to death. But I could still think and move, and with all my strength, I forced some girders apart – I never felt the pain of my burned hands until later – and burst out of my prison. I fell full length on cool wet grass … I can't explain how I survived. All I can say is that my gondola was 100 metres from the tail cone and the tail structure broke the force of my fall, while the bow remained intact and did not collapse on me entirely.[4]

Astonishingly, he then was helped by British civilians to drag another man, horribly burnt but still alive, out of the wreckage of the control car.

There were also hazards for the ground crews who manhandled the airships in and out of their sheds, and marshalled them on the ground. Zeppelins were controlled by men holding on to ropes on the ground. In marginal, gusting wind conditions, control was sometimes tenuous. A man holding on to a rope could suddenly find himself being lifted into the air. His decision whether and when to let go or not was not a straightforward one. He and his comrades were charged with controlling the airship and if people wantonly let go of their ropes when they were lifted a foot or two in the air, then they would fail. So the pressure from peers and superiors to hang on was strong. A quick lift a few feet off the ground and down again was fine. But a few feet might, without warning, rapidly become quite a lot of feet. When one is, say, 20 feet in the air, does one hang on in the hope that the Zeppelin will come down again quickly, or does one let go risking possible injury? From time to time, men made the wrong decision and found themselves gripping for dear life to a rope hundreds of feet in the air beyond the help of those in the airship or on the ground. Unless the airship came down to earth again very quickly, they lived only as long as the strength of their arms.

It was not only Zeppelin ground crews who were faced with such risks, for similar incidents also happened with their British counterparts:

On 20 July 1917, SS39 [a submarine scouting balloon] was being walked back to its shed after an instructional flight, the wind being no more that 4 to 5 mph. An up-current of extreme violence caught and dragged her out of the hands of the landing party, who nearly all let go. The Officer Commanding, Wing Commander CM Waterlow, Petty Officer MG Collins and Aircraftman S Lightstone held on to their ropes and were carried upwards to a great height. All three eventually dropped off the ship [sic] and fell to their deaths.[5]

In a close small community such as the German Naval Airship Division, the losses hurt hard. The sight of their fellows crashing in flames haunted many men's dreams. But such was the fragility of these monsters that they were always prone to accidents. The description of one accident is somehow representative of many others. On one occasion during the night, a Zeppelin had become stern heavy through loss of gas in one of her rear gas cells. Her crew dropped rear ballast and moved fuel and bombs to the fore end of the craft. At dawn, she descended through thick fog to try and get her bearings with the ground. Through a sudden change in air temperature, the gas expanded and she became nose heavy. The engines were set at full speed to try and increase the speed of air flowing over her control surfaces and give her dynamic lift. At a height of 200 to 300 feet, she broke out of the fog and the crew saw the ice-covered estuary of the River Weser below them. The engines were immediately stopped and forward ballast was dropped. The bombs that had been moved forward could not be dropped because at this height they would have probably destroyed the airship. The beast continued downwards until the control car smashed hard on to the ice. One crew member fell out and was able to make his way to shore in spite of an injured foot. The airship then shot back up into the air to 3,300 feet, but since the damaged control car threatened to tear itself off and the escape ladder to the body of the airship had been smashed, the lives of the men still inside the control car were hanging by a thin thread indeed. Gas was released and the Zeppelin came down again to the ice. The control car crew were now able somehow to climb up into the airship, but up she went again this time into bright sunlight above the fog. The wrecked control car soon fell away. With no charts, no radio and no controls, the aviators were soon lost. By 1300 hrs a range of unidentified mountains loomed above the clouds. With the gas warming up in the sun and the loss of the control gondola, the airship continued to ascend so the crew resorted to trying to control her by valving individual gas bags. They managed to get her to descend once more to 600 feet when she suddenly became stern heavy again. They dropped their last ballast but to no avail. She crashed through tree tops, ripped away some power lines, somehow without sparking off the hydrogen, and crashed on the ice of the River Aller. The wind caught her and drove her on to the river bank where she broke in two. Astonishingly no lives were lost.

Anyone who flew in these machines was brave, but especial respect must be reserved for the men who climbed up the ladder through the frame and took their station on the roof of the envelope as machine gunners to defend against attack from above. Like the rear gunners in aircraft of a later era, they were isolated from their friends and would probably be the first to die in a fire. Their life expectancy was not good if things went wrong.

And then there was the 'sub-cloud car'. This was a small streamlined pod – the prototype was a converted butter barrel – which, when suspended in clear air up to 5,000 feet below the Zeppelin, allowed an observer connected by telephone to the control car to direct the airship hidden in the clouds above. It performed the function of an inverted periscope and, with its steel cable and winch, it weighed half a ton. It also added to the risk of lightning strikes. One of these devices and its winch broke away from its parent craft and crashed to earth near Colchester, Essex many thousands of feet below. No one was found in it although why the machine would have been lowered empty is not clear. Perhaps it simply fell off or maybe it was manned and the body never found. There was evidence that a desperate attempt had been made to jam the runaway winch with a crowbar. This sub-cloud car is now hanging from the ceiling of the Imperial War Museum in London. When looking at it, nothing can impart the sense of the precarious fragility of life for aviators more completely than the thought of this flimsy, helpless toy suspended several thousand feet beneath a Zeppelin, itself many thousands of feet up in the air.

The German Navy experimented with sub-cloud cars and their commander, Peter Strasser, took part in the trials. In April 1916, he was being lowered in a sub-cloud car from a Zeppelin.

> About 300 feet down, as the winch slowly but steadily paid out cable, the stabilizing fin of the car became entangled with the Zeppelin's radio antenna – a weighted wire hanging free from the aft gondola. It caught the car and tilted it upside down. The cable, meanwhile, continued unravelling from the winch and was bellying in a slack loop below Strasser, who saved himself only by clinging to the sides of the car. Suddenly the antenna gave way, sending the car and its passenger plunging until brought up at the end of the cable with a violent sickening jolt.[6]

The German Navy eventually rejected sub-cloud cars, but the Army used them operationally.

What kind of extraordinary man would volunteer to descend in the sub-cloud car nearly a mile below the airship at the end of a cable? The answer is: a man who smoked. Unsurprisingly, smoking was strictly forbidden in the main body and gondolas of Zeppelins. Apparently the prospect of a comforting drag to brighten the long dark hours aloft was sufficient incentive to induce some brave souls to volunteer for this uniquely isolated and hazardous duty.

Even more surprising is the fact that the German Navy did not issue parachutes to their airship crews. The German Army had a more pragmatic outlook and their Zeppelin crews usually had recourse to parachutes, although they do not seem to have used them very often. But as with the Navy, their dirigible airships came to earth out of control with remarkable frequency, even in peacetime. In wartime, once searchlights, anti-aircraft guns and effective fighter aircraft were developed, they were brought down in flames again and again with fatal results for their crews. And yet, 'no live parachute drop was ever made from a naval airship, in an emergency or otherwise.'[7] The explanation offered is that they were carried for a short while in early 1917, but 'because parachutes for 20 men weighed a total of 365 lbs, they were soon discarded because of their weight'.[8] This is unconvincing to say the least. Of the Zeppelins of 1914, the useful payload available for crew, spare parts, stores, water, ballast, petrol, oil, armaments and bombs was around 20,000lb. A year later this had grown to 30,000lb, and by the end of 1917 these machines were capable of lifting over 70,000lb – over 30 tons. The fact that 365lb could not be allocated for potentially life-saving parachutes for the crew is a bleak statement about the priorities of the day. Peter Strasser, the commander of the Naval Airship Division, is reported to have scoffed at the Army for carrying parachutes instead of bombs, implying that the Army Zeppelin crews' commitment to the destruction of London was less than their commitment to getting home again in one piece. It was rumoured that vials of quick-acting poison were issued to naval aircrew to give them an instant merciful alternative to death by fire,[9] although this is contradicted by at least one verbatim account.[10]

Servicemen and women risk death from many causes, none of which is pleasant. But to be trapped in a burning aircraft, or a burning airship, at 10,000 or 20,000 feet, a craft which might take some minutes to descend to certain death, must be to endure an especial torment which beggars the imagination. And yet officialdom on both sides condemned unnecessarily many hundreds of their airmen to death in this way. One is reluctantly forced to the conclusion that life was indeed cheap in the halls of power in the early twentieth century.

As with the Royal Naval Air Service, the German Naval Air Service attracted some outstanding men. The driving force behind the Zeppelin operations over the North Sea and over Britain was Korvettenkapitän Peter

Strasser. The equivalent rank of a commander or lieutenant colonel, he, like his counterpart Commander Samson on the British side, exercised authority and responsibility far above that which his rank might suggest. He became Chief of the German Naval Airship Division in 1913 and remained in command throughout the war until his death in August 1918. He picked it up after the disasters of 1913, when two out of the three existing naval Zeppelins and their crews were lost in accidents, and with remarkable persistence and determination, built it into the powerful and significant force that it became. A man of great energy, enthusiasm and persuasive charm, Strasser was a technical innovator, a brilliant organiser and an outstanding leader. He was constantly devising new and better ways of operating, and as these threw up technical and tactical problems, he devised innovative, practical solutions. Under his leadership, the German Naval Airship Division pioneered long-distance and high-altitude aviation. Again and again he went out with his men on their lonely, dangerous missions, and again and again, they drew encouragement and strength from his company and personal example. Strasser sustained the will and the morale of his men through five years' terrible attrition. Between October 1912 and August 1918, a total of seventy-two dirigible airships was commissioned into the German Naval Airship Division. Of this number, only seventeen survived. Twenty-nine were destroyed in accidents, many of which were fatal, and twenty-six were lost to enemy action.

As the commander of any small elite arm must be, Strasser was utterly convinced, and convincing, of the value of his command and the importance of its contribution to the greater war effort. Indeed, one might argue that he was too convincing. He was consumed with the conviction that the Zeppelin could be the instrument whereby Germany would win the war. He was grossly over-optimistic about what his people were achieving. They consistently overestimated the damage they were doing and Strasser believed them. Yet the greatest raid of all, with sixteen airships, achieved no more than the destruction of a gasholder, damage to some houses and killed four people. This was also for the loss of one airship. In spite of this, Strasser was still telling Admiral Scheer that 'England can be overcome by means of airships, inasmuch as the country will be deprived of the means of existence through increasingly extensive destruction of cities, factory complexes, dockyards, harbour works with warships and merchant ships lying therein, railroads etc.'[11] Strasser was trying to achieve, with eighteen airships, what the Allies in the Second World War manifestly failed to do to Germany with vastly greater and more capable resources at their disposal – to bring a major, modern industrial country to surrender by bombing from the air.

Peter Strasser's optimism in the face of the evidence was almost pathological. After the first Zepplin raid on UK in January 1915, the German press might be excused for writing: 'The moat has been bridged. Our glorious airships will persevere in their attacks on the enemy asylum and every bomb will be an arrow piercing the coward's gut. Our aerial avengers will smash the island citadel.' [12] The problem was that Strasser, who should have known better, believed it, and continued to believe it throughout the war. In spite of his demonstrable failure to deliver British defeat from the air, he even seriously proposed to Admiral Scheer in July 1918 that he start a bombing campain against the United States.[13]

Eventually he conceded that the chief value of the airship raids was in the resources that they forced the British to deploy to protect against them. In this he was probably right. In early 1917, over 17,000 men were engaged in anti-aircraft activities and a further 2,000 men were supporting the twelve Royal Flying Corps squadrons that were committed to air defence. These were resources that were not being sent to France to fight the German Army. And yet measured against this must be the cost of building and maintaining the Naval Airship Division, which has been estimated as equivalent to maintaining two army divisions.[14] In May 1917, the Kaiser finally agreed that Zeppelins would be better used by concentrating their efforts in support of the High Seas Fleet, although the raids were to continue right through to the final weeks of the war.

Peter Strasser was undoubtedly one of the outstanding junior commanders of the war on either side. Yet his service was a paradox. He was a brilliant commander but had limited strategic insight. The resolution, charm and powers of persuasion which were part of his strength as a leader were also ingredients of his failure. Had he been less resolute, less persuasive and charming, maybe his masters would have felt more inclined to give him firmer and perhaps more fruitful strategic direction. Had a lesser man been in command of the German Naval Airship Division, it might have played a more crucial part in the outcome of the conflict, and his death in the final Zeppelin raid of all, in August 1918, while tragic, was somehow all of a piece with the part that he performed on the stage of war.

Notes

1 Royle, Trevor, *The Flowers of the Forest*, Birlinn, 2007, p. 213.

2 Robinson, Douglas, *The Zeppelin in Combat*, Foulis & Co., 1971, p. 100.

3 Ibid., p. 102.

4 Account of Heinrich Ellerkamm, quoted by Douglas Robinson, *The Zeppelin in Combat*, p. 232.

5 Haslam, E.B., *The History of Royal Air Force Cranwell*, HMSO, 1982, pp. 11-12.

6 Norman, Aaron, *The Great Air War 1914-1918*, Macmillan, 1968, p. 353.

7 Robinson, *The Zeppelin in Combat*, p. 366.

8 Ibid., p. 366.

9 Norman, *The Great Air War 1914-1918*, p. 366.

10 Account of Heinrich Ellerkamm, quoted by Douglas Robinson, *The Zeppelin in Combat*, p. 232.

11 Robinson, *The Zeppelin in Combat*, p. 165.

12 Norman, *The Great Air War 1914-1918*, p. 350.

13 Ibid., p. 409.

14 Ibid., p. 400.

Chapter 7

Long Shadows of the Past

In 1909, the commander of Italy's balloon battalion, Colonel Giulio Douhet, had a vision of future air power which was as stunning in the clarity of its perception as it was unfashionable and repugnant to those who first read it.

No doubt Douhet had read H.G. Wells's sensationalist, fanciful science fiction book, *The War in the Air*, which had been published around the same time, but whereas Wells foresaw a new dark age in which technology had outstripped man's ability to control it, Douhet applied a methodical, informed, military mind to thinking how flight might affect future wars. Looking at the nascent technology under his command, and observing what was happening around him, he foresaw that the land battle would be changed for ever by intervention from the air. Not only would soldiers at the front be bombed, but their lines of communication would be interrupted, their supply depots would be destroyed, the factories that made their munitions would be razed, and their families at home would be terrorised from the air. He envisaged this being done, not merely by an arm of the Navy or the Army, but by a separate service specifically established and equipped to deliver industrial destruction from the air. The natural corollary was that fighting air machines would be developed to attack and defend other air machines, and that supremacy in the air would be the deciding factor in a future war.

He believed that, instead of concentrating solely upon the destruction of the enemy's armies and navies, it would be much more cost effective to neutralise his ability to wage war; to destroy his communications, his factories, his seat of government, and above all the will of his population to sustain the fight. He had no illusions about chivalry in war. He knew that such a strategy would mean wholesale killing of innocents, but he believed that, since this would bring about the cessation of hostilities more quickly than any other means, the end would justify the carnage.

He earned no friends by his brilliance. He was mocked, vilified, court-martialled and sent to jail. But by 1918, both sides in the First World War had, tacitly or by default, accepted the validity of his theories. And in the

Second World War, his vision became a central plank of Allied policy. It also has echoes which resonate through to our own time. The Blitz, the Allied destruction of German cities, the dropping of atomic bombs on Japan, the NATO bombing campaign in Kosovo – Giulio Douhet foresaw them all. And all this from the commander of an Italian balloon battalion in 1909.

It is now widely assumed that some of Douhet's views have not stood up well to the test of time. He wrote before effective air defence was possible. He also greatly underestimated the weight, strength and number of bombs and aircraft necessary to achieve the levels of destruction that he foresaw, and he overestimated the effect such destruction would have on the morale of the civilian population. If any country's morale was ever going to be broken by bombing, it should surely have been Germany's in the Second World War, but in spite of the carpet bombing and firestorm raids designed to terrorise and 'de-house' the German people, it was not a breakdown of civilian morale that led to the defeat of Germany. Ground and air forces had to defeat the German Army in the field. Nevertheless, Douhet achieved vindication of a sort when Japan surrendered at a stroke when two cities were destroyed by nuclear weapons in August 1945. He might not have foreseen nuclear weapons, but the mass destruction they wrought was precisely the precondition he envisaged for civil collapse and the suing for peace.

Whatever the modern view of Douhet's ideas may be, in the early years of the twentieth century, his shade was an ever-present influence in the halls where men deliberated upon air policy. His shadow can be seen there still.

The single-minded dedication to reconnaissance of the first leaders of the Royal Flying Corps was also to cast a long shadow. The performance of the early Royal Flying Corps was dominated by the urge to convince their masters that military aviation had a useful role to play. So much effort seems to have gone in this direction that little thought was given to matters beyond the tactical support of the Army on the ground. When the Royal Flying Corps was forced to come to terms with the new roles demanded by the stalemate of trench warfare, they found themselves with unsuitable aircraft, inadequate equipment and poorly trained pilots. Their slow stable machines were ill-suited for fighting, or for carrying observers, cameras, radios, machine guns or bombs. Instead of doctrine, training, tactics and machines stemming from a thorough analysis of the operational requirement, they had to resort to the gallantry and self-sacrifice of their pilots.

No such accusation could be made of the Royal Naval Air Service, which was inspired and encouraged on to wider, greater things by its flamboyant and visionary leaders, Churchill and Sueter. It was the Navy who first developed more powerful and capable machines which, again and again, they were prevailed upon to hand over to the Army who were discovering that they were suffering for the want of them.[1] Today's maritime aviation, in all its complexities, can trace its genesis to this period, and after Friedrichshafen and Cuxhaven they went on to harry new German installations in occupied Belgium from their base in Dunkirk, even though much of their resources were diverted to the Dardanelles. Attacks against the submarine base at Ostend met with indifferent success, but in June 1915, two out of the three Zeppelins based near Brussels were destroyed in one night forcing the Germans to relocate their airships back in Germany.

While the Army remained firmly focussed on the tactical benefits of air support, the Navy saw their air arm essentially as an offensive weapon and appreciated its strategic value.

The Dardanelles, resource shortages and Churchill's resignation constrained naval plans for the remainder of 1915, but by the end of the year they had started talking to the French with a view to establishing an Allied bombing force to attack vital German industries such as chemical and steel works within range of bases in French territory. In early 1916, plans had matured to the point whereby an Allied wing of some 100 bombers was envisaged to be based at Luxeuil, 25 miles north-west of Belfort.

Meanwhile, Army demands for more and more aircraft in support of the land battles in 1916 absorbed the greater part of British aircraft production capacity. David Henderson was now at the War Office and Trenchard was commanding the Royal Flying Corps in France. Both believed in the priority of reconnaissance, air fighting and tactical bombing. Strategic bombing of the enemy's cities or war industries was of little importance to them. In the inter-Service battle for resources, and in the struggle between the Services to support their respective conceptions of air power, the Army view prevailed. The growth of the strategic Navy wing at Luxeuil was starved, delayed and eventually disbanded, and, in April 1917, the resources were turned over to supporting the Army.

Then, barely a month later, with heavier-than-air powered machines supplanting Zeppelins after their brief meteoric predominance, the Germans started bombing Britain with Gotha aircraft. They first raided Shorncliffe and Folkestone. They next attacked Shoeburyness and Sheerness, and bombed London the following month, and then London again in early July. There was an outburst of public outrage and indignation. People had more or less come to terms with Zeppelins making things go bump in the night and they knew – and occasionally saw – that from time to time they were clawed out of the sky in flaming pyres. But this was different. In four raids, these aircraft had killed about half the number of people that the Zeppelins had killed in two years. By later standards, the damage and loss of life was a mere bagatelle but these raiders had come across the Channel in broad daylight, bombed, killed and injured innocent civilians in London and elsewhere, and returned home largely unscathed, in spite of the efforts of home defence squadrons. What on earth were our Forces doing to stop them? Why weren't they inflicting similar horrors on the Germans? More critically: was this the beginning of a far greater offensive? Was this the start of a Douhet-like onslaught on Great Britain?

As part of its response to these unexpected and ineffectively opposed raids, the government asked General Jan Christiaan Smuts to study British air policy generally and to make recommendations. Believing erroneously that a substantial surplus of aircraft would soon become available, and also perhaps influenced by being present in London when the second raid on that city took place, he recommended that a single air service with its own air ministry be formed to deliver Douhet-like destruction to Germany via a long-range bomber force.

The British had to set about devastating Germany before the Germans devastated Britain, and this was best done by a service independent of the parochial demands of the Navy or the Army. These proposals were not met with universal approval, especially when doubts about the likely surplus of aircraft arose, but coming as they did when public hysteria and government panic were at their most frenetic, Smuts's work achieved a momentum which has lasted to this day. A single service with its own ministry was duly formed, a strategic bombing force reconstituted, and retaliatory raids conducted on German industries and infrastructure.

Smuts was not necessarily wrong in his assessment of the future decisive nature of strategic airpower. He was merely, like the science fiction writer H.G. Wells, a few decades ahead of his time. But ahead of his time he was, and the bombing force that was established never got anywhere near to achieving the decisive result that he envisaged – and it is probably true to say that the Royal Air Force, which was formally founded on 1 April 1918, was born out of a governmental knee-jerk reaction to public hysteria, and a misplaced faith in an Italian prophet.

Furthermore, there was a number of conflicting agendas buried in the gestation of the Royal Air Force and it did not have an easy birth. David Henderson, who had supported Smuts with his proposals and had been instrumental in turning them into fact, was no supporter of strategic bombing. But he felt that resource allocation and policy could only be sensibly formulated by a powerful independent body, and so he swallowed his reservations. Trenchard shared Henderson's view and was in no way convinced either that Germany was about to inflict destruction on an industrial scale on Britain, or that trying to inflict industrial destruction on Germany was the appropriate response. He was also reluctant to set about forming a new independent service in the middle of a war. However, he too accepted the political situation. When the first Air Council was established in early 1918, Henderson was made Vice President, and Trenchard became Chief of the Air Staff. Lord Rothermere was the Secretary of State for Air and immediately fell out with Trenchard. Trenchard resigned within two months, his resignation taking effect twelve days after the formal birth of his new command. Rothermere resigned a month later. Frederick Sykes, the bombing advocate and the man whom everyone hated, but who was probably the most able of them all, was retrieved from outer darkness and was made Chief of the Air Staff in place of Trenchard. On hearing this, Henderson promptly resigned too.

Having been instrumental in strangling the Royal Naval Air Service's endeavours to advance an Allied strategic bombing force, it was no small irony that Trenchard should then be appointed to command the Independent Force, the force that finally took the strategic bombing campaign to Germany.

By April 1918, the 1914 exploits of the early pilots and their flying machines made of linen-covered wooden frames, held together with piano wire, had been developed into a completely new service created alongside the Royal Navy and the Army to deliver applied violence in and from the air: the Royal Air Force. This new air force had established within it an element which was the predecessor to Bomber Command of the Second World War: the Independent Force, a force within an air force. By the end of the war, the recognisable seeds of the massive structures that evolved in the Second World War, designed to pound Germany's industrial production, her civil infrastructures, her war machinery and her people into destruction and submission, were all in place.

Bombs with armoured noses designed for maximum penetration and size of crater were in service. Incendiary bombs, gas bombs, fragmentation and anti-personnel bombs were all in regular use. Aircraft and bomb-sight development had continued apace (but not parachute development), and although the war finished before it could see active service, a four-engined bomber capable of striking Berlin from a British base was in an advanced state of production. Properly prepared and drained mounting airfields with fuel tanks and distribution pipelines had been built. These airfields had ammunition and bomb dumps, and railways to supply them, and were protected by airfield defence anti-aircraft guns. By 1918, the weight of the bombs had grown tenfold and the numbers of aircraft too had multiplied. Air wings of no less than ten or twelve aircraft flew on these latter raids, using tactics and formations designed to afford maximum protection. They conducted night as well as day raids, and faced a coordinated anti-aircraft defence network of fighter aircraft, guns, balloons and aircraft observers on the ground. They bombed railway yards, chemical plants, machine and ordnance factories, power stations, and iron and steel works. They even bombed the machinery at the head of mines. On 18 October 1918, Charles Collet's successors dropped 3 tons of explosives on Kaiserlauten – a hundred and eightyfold increase on Collet's load.

During the First World War, the Independent Force of bombers was never more than a small part of the whole British air effort, and it was certainly not the war-winning instrument that was envisaged by Smuts – and Douhet. Its effect on Germany's ability to wage war probably was no greater than that of the German Zeppelin and Gotha raids on Britain. In other words, the expenditure and commitment of resources required to defend against it was the greater part of its value. Nevertheless, doctrine, training, equipment and infrastructure, all shaped by hard experience, had come together to forge a strategic bomber force which, if the war had gone on much longer, could have played an important part in defeating Germany. Furthermore, much detailed scientific operational research and analysis had been conducted to determine what could and could not be done, and which targets should be hit by which bombs in what number to achieve the greatest effect. All this had happened in four short years and it had all grown from those raids on Düsseldorf, Friedrichshafen and Cuxhaven in 1914.

And yet, even with all this experience of bombing and of being bombed, British corporate memory let much of this precious knowledge evaporate between the wars. Between 1918 and 1939, the presumed power of the strategic bomber came to dominate British defence thinking. It became received wisdom that the bomber would always get through and bring about the result that Douhet said it would: a breakdown of the enemy's war-fighting capability and his will to fight. This born-again absolute faith in the bomber was not based on any experience or scientific exploration. The manifold complexities of target selection, the effects of weather and pilot fatigue, long-range navigation, night flying, defence against fighters, target identification, battle-damage assessment, bombing accuracy, and weight and types of bomb remained largely unexplored. No scientific studies were carried out which assessed just how many bombers, carrying what tonnage of bombs, might be required to have a high degree of expectancy of success. All these and more had been worked on by 1918, but many of the lessons learned with blood and treasure between 1914 and 1918 accumulated dust on forgotten shelves.[2] Rather, the faith in the bomber owed more to the earlier notion that explosives dropped from the air were somehow vastly more destructive than those delivered by ground-based weapons, than it owed to operational analysis and exercise.

A generation later, a similar faith was placed in nuclear weapons, but in that case, at least the belief was based on what had been experienced at Hiroshima and Nagasaki. In the 1930s, that faith was premature at best. Moreover, in the nuclear age, it was deemed that substantial modern land and naval forces – conventional forces – were superfluous. So it was in the inter-war years. The bomber would settle it. However, politicians and senior airmen between the wars, having nailed their colours to the bomber, did very little to equip the country with a bomber force that had even a whisper of a chance of living up to their hopes or expectations. Consequently, in 1939, British bombers were incapable of penetrating German defences by day, or of finding and hitting precision targets by night, and the British strategic bombing efforts in the first part of the Second World War were pitifully inadequate.

One must also ask how far the shadows of 1912 stretched into the 1930s. When the air arms of the Army and the Navy came together to form the new Royal Air Force in 1918, the Royal Flying Corps was by far the bigger of the two, and so the Army influence was predominant. Nevertheless, strategic bombing was a child of the Navy. Much of the operational analysis and research had been conducted by Lord Tiverton, a brilliant but relatively junior naval officer. The complexities of navigation and long-distance flying at night were more akin to naval skills rather than army ones, and so the experience and corporate memory of what was and what was not possible had faded, as it always tends to do if not jogged and revitalised by events.

Churchill became head of both the War and Air Ministries in 1919. He recalled Hugh Trenchard, the passed-over infantry major who turned airman at the age of thirty-nine, to become Chief of the Air Staff once more. Trenchard remained in that post for the next ten years. Although, like Henderson, he was convinced of the rightness of having an independent air service, like Henderson, he was not convinced of the virtues of strategic bombing. He, who had commanded the Independent Force, and had been responsible for delivering airborne death and destruction, seems to have had grave doubts about what his command had achieved. He felt that the bombing had had very little effect on Germany's ability to fight. He believed that German morale had not been adversely affected at all. In fact, he believed it had been stiffened by the bombing. He declared that 'a more gigantic waste of effort and personnel there has never been in any war.'[3]

Trenchard had a Herculean task in creating and sustaining the new Service in the face of the budgetary constraints and the massive force reductions that came with the end of war. He also had to fight off attempts by the Army and the Navy to break it up again. This he did manfully and successfully, but he needed any tool, every argument that he could lay his hands on. He certainly has an irrefutable claim to be the champion of the Royal Air Force, if not its father. But could it be that in his struggles with the other Services to preserve the life of Henderson's child, he over-egged the strategic case for air power, and had little appetite or energy left over for ensuring that British defence policy between the wars, based on Douhet's theory, had any real substance? Did form shape function rather than vice versa? So, perhaps Trenchard too played his part in allowing the hope of the strategic potency of the bomber to become the father of the thought.

The ghost of Douhet's theory has yet to be exorcised to this day. In an environment where Western democracies are unwilling to accept anything but the shortest of casualty lists, the notion that technology and machines can do one's dirty work for one is more beguiling and tempting than ever. There remains, even after a century of experience, a pervasive residual notion that in one form or another, bombing from the air is the ultimate persuader, the ultimate tool of coercion. The outlandish idea current in some quarters in 1912 that explosives delivered from the air are somehow endowed with a destructive power far greater than if delivered from land, still seems to have some life in it.

In the late 1990s, President Slobodan Milosevic of Serbia resolved to expel the Muslims of Albanian extraction from the Serbian province of Kosovo. In pursuit of Slav ethnic purity, his police and army set about terrorising, raping and forcibly expelling large numbers of non-Slav people who had lived in Kosovo for generations. The North Atlantic Treaty Organisation decided that such behaviour was not acceptable in a civilised Europe and tried to persuade him to stop. Negotiations were unsuccessful so NATO considered what they might do in the form of a demonstration to illustrate what might happen if he did not comply. An air exercise was conducted over neighbouring Albania. The implicit message was that, unless you behave, we will bomb you. Milosevic did not want to be bombed, but he sensed either that NATO would not have the political will to put their threat into action, or if they did, he would have finished his work in achieving ethnic purity in Kosovo before they mustered the will to fly. So he carried on with his repugnant work regardless.

A year later, in the final year of the twentieth century, NATO applied Douhet's theory and started bombing Serbia. It wasn't pure Douhet, of course. The complete devastation he advocated was out of the question. But weapons of great precision and accuracy were applied in large numbers to targets carefully chosen to hurt Milosevic and his machinery of repression, and to shape his will. It was the clear intention to force Serbia to comply with NATO's demands through a campaign of bombing alone.

In spite of all the evidence from the twentieth century suggesting that Douhet was mistaken on this point, NATO hoped to succeed by applying air power in isolation. There was no intent to use ground troops. Indeed, a ground campaign was specifically ruled out from the start. The air campaign was initiated in the belief that it would preclude a costly ground campaign. Air power alone would be sufficient.

Led by the German general Klaus Naumann, who as a child had seen at first hand what bombing could do – and could not do – most senior military advisors were quite clear that bombing alone would not force compliance. It would only succeed if conducted in conjunction with the real threat of a land campaign. But NATO had no stomach for a land operation and Milosevic knew it. This military advice was put to one side and the bombing started.

And so, the late-twentieth-century aviators rediscovered that political and moral scruples interfered with their freedom to hit the targets that they really wanted to hit. Like their brothers at the other end of the century, they found that weather was an important limiting factor in locating and identifying targets, and assessing battle damage. Like their predecessors, from Pemberton Billing and Strasser onwards, they tended to overestimate the damage they had done, and the effect they were having on the enemy. In spite of the latest miracles of surveillance technology, they sometimes hit the wrong targets and discovered that the Serbs were able to deceive them and hide precious assets. They discovered that precision guided weapons needed equally precise intelligence which ultimately could only be provided by people on the ground. They needed to see in real time: 'what was underneath the clouds and inside buildings. We need to know whether the men on the tractors and inside the buses were soldiers or civilians. We will want to know whether trucks are carrying food or weapons. We will want to know who is in the underground facility: civilians or military, families or opposing leaders.'[4] Lack of all these limited the effectiveness of the air campaign, but it was also discovered that in spite of hitting many of the targets more than once, this had little effect in bending the will of Milosevic and his repressive regime. In short, the bombing campaign didn't work. When this became clear, NATO finally faced up to the necessity of a ground campaign, and planning and preparation for such a campaign finally began in earnest. Milosevic, realising that at last NATO meant business, agreed to NATO's terms.

And so, ninety years after H.G. Wells and Giulio Douhet first aired their ideas, in spite of computers, stealth bombers, smart missiles, precision guided weapons, weapons of mass destruction and surveillance technology of the greatest sophistication, it was discovered yet again that morale, courage, endurance and human ingenuity remain everything.

Notes

1 Raleigh, Walter *Official History of the War: The War in the Air*,vol I., OUP, 1922,p. 472.

2 Jones, Neville, *The Origins of Strategic Bombing*, William Kimber, 1973,pp. 208-9.

3 Rennles, Keith, *Independent Force: The War Diary of the Daylight Squadrons of the Independent Air Force, June–November 1918*, Grub Street, 2002, p. 201.

4 Clark, Wesley, *Waging Modern War*, Public Affairs, 2001, p. 437.

Postscript

Winston Churchill never did learn to fly. It grieved him sorely to have to stop his training just short of taking his flying certificate in 1912, but his flying exploits were a source of deep anxiety to his pregnant wife, and his sense of duty to her and his family was even stronger than his wish to fly.[1] Given the high incidence of fatal crashes among early pilots, we can be thankful to her for this and her many other fruitful influences upon him. He tried to qualify again when he became the joint Secretary of State for Air and for War in 1919. But, as Roy Jenkins describes him, Churchill was not one of nature's pilots.[2] Undeterred by one crash landing at Buc near Paris, he survived another a month later during an evening flight at Croydon. As his aeroplane headed earthwards out of control, he thought he was going to die, but in spite of heavy bruising and a badly scratched face, he drove off to London the same evening to preside over a House of Commons dinner for General Pershing, the commander of American forces in France.[3] He was finally persuaded to abandon his aerial ambitions, to much widespread relief, not least among his instructors. The fact that he never qualified as a pilot didn't stop him wearing Royal Air Force pilot's wings during the Second World War. Given the all-important influence he had as a politician over early British aviation, it would be difficult to begrudge him this little vanity.

Churchill's subsequent career needs no further elaboration on these pages, but Commodore Murray Sueter, with whom he worked so productively, continued to turn his own inventive mind and restless personality to improving naval aviation. Having been an early torpedo specialist, and having played an important part in the development of the seaplane, it was a natural step for Sueter to combine the two and lead in the development of the first torpedo-bomber. The first successful torpedo attack on a ship was conducted as a result of this work in 1915. When Churchill left the Admiralty in 1915, Sueter lost his most loyal and influential sponsor. With the expansion of the Royal Naval Air Service, an admiral was made the Director of the Admiralty Air Department, but it was not Sueter – he was moved sideways as superintendent of aircraft construction. Churchill had known that, to get the best out of Sueter, his headstrong personality should be tolerated and he should be given as much leeway as possible. His new masters were not so indulgent. After a difference of opinion in 1917 Sueter was sent to southern Italy to command the Royal Naval Air Service in that theatre.

Sueter always felt that he had not been accorded due recognition for the part he had played in the development of the tank and, somewhat injudiciously, wrote to the King on the subject. This did not endear him to the Admiralty and he was relieved of his command and retired, aged forty-eight. He was, however, promoted to rear admiral shortly after being placed on the retired list. Sueter entered Parliament in 1921, taking Noel Pemberton Billing's seat, and in 1934 he was knighted for services to the Conservative Party. He remained a member until 1945. He published his own account of the evolution of the tank and his part in it, and another self-justificatory, rambling polemic castigating those men in senior places who did not agree with his views on aviation matters. Given the neglect of British maritime aviation in the 1920s and 1930s, it is difficult not to concede that he had a point.

Between the wars, long after the Zeppelin had ceased to exercise the minds of politicians and military men, Britain continued to develop a fleet of aircraft carriers. The requirement was no longer driven by the Zeppelin but by the need to police an empire depending upon the sea lines for its communications. However, in 1918, the new Royal Air Force took over responsibility for all military air capability and, in the face of competition with the bomber as the means of taking the war to the enemy, maritime aviation found itself the runt of the litter. In addition, naval officers out of touch with developments in naval aviation asked the Air Ministry for designs that reflected the priorities of reconnaissance and spotting, rather than those of fighting and bombing. In that lamentable inter-war period of post-war exhaustion, disillusionment, economic parsimony and betrayal by appeasement, the Fleet Air Arm fell behind both its land-based counterpart and other navies. By the outbreak of the next world conflict, its main offensive aircraft was the Fairey Swordfish, a biplane with a maximum speed that was only 40 mph greater than that of the Sopwith Tabloid of 1913. It was left to the Americans and the Japanese to build on the lessons learnt by the British, and they created carrier fleets with modern, highly potent, versatile aircraft which were soon struggling for supremacy in the Pacific Ocean.

Sueter watched all this unfold with frustration and sadness, but his place in history as a key driver of progress in early British naval aviation is secure.

David Henderson, ex-Argyll and Sutherland Highlander and the true 'father of the Royal Air Force', became the head of the Red Cross in Geneva after the war. His only son, Ian, was one of the first casualties of the new Royal Air Force when he was killed in a flying accident at Turnberry in Ayrshire seven weeks after the Force's formation. David Henderson outlived the birth of his intellectual child and the death of his biological child by only three years. He died in 1921 aged fifty-nine and was buried alongside his son in Girvan, not far from the airfield where the boy was killed.

Frederick Sykes, erstwhile cavalry trooper, pilot and Royal Marine colonel, and a 'brilliant officer with a singularly luminous mind',[4] but a man whom Henderson and Trenchard had found it impossible to work with, remained Chief of the Air Staff until the end of the war. He did much valuable work in this period to establish the new Service, work which his successor and arch enemy, Trenchard, was quick to build upon and equally quick to obscure. Sykes was moved on by Churchill in 1919 and became a Member of Parliament. He married the daughter of Andrew Bonar Law who was briefly to be Prime Minister between Lloyd George and Stanley Baldwin, and he became Governor of Bombay. He died in 1954.

Charles Samson, who lit the love of flying in Winston Churchill, who did so much at the practical and tactical levels to develop aircraft, equipment, procedures, doctrine and training, and who led the formations that conducted the earliest raids, did not become the founding father figure he should have been. He won the Distinguished Service Order twice, and personally experimented and broke new ground with bombing, communications, flying from ships, night flying and many other hazardous unknowns of early maritime aviation. He thrived in the chaotic, unpredictable circumstances of war and saw much action in Europe and in the Dardanelles, but was much more at home in the air than behind a desk. After the war, he made a number of record-breaking flights but his restless, freelancing, buccaneering spirit was not conducive to a successful peacetime career. He died of a heart attack aged forty-seven in 1931, but his legacy is visible in every modern navy today.

After his attack on the Zeppelin shed in Düsseldorf in 1914, Charles Collet was destined to have an active, but sadly short, flying career. He was shot down twice in France early the following year. On the first occasion, he crash-landed between the British and German lines but managed to make his way safely across the British lines on foot. On the second occasion, he was over German-held territory when his engine was destroyed by shrapnel. He glided towards the Belgian lines, being shot at by both friend and foe, but was able to land on the right side of the Belgian trenches. The Belgians mistook him for a German and took him prisoner. The following year Collet deployed with the Royal Naval Air Service to the Dardanelles theatre. In June 1915, he was flying an aeroplane in which his observer, Major Hogg, managed to shoot the engine of a German aircraft with a rifle and bring it down over the Gallipoli peninsula. Charles Collet was killed in an aircraft accident on the island of Imbros two months later. As he burned to death trapped in the wreckage of his aircraft, Chief Petty

Officer Michael Keogh ran into the flames and succeeded in dragging him free, but was himself overcome by burns. Keogh survived and was awarded the Albert Medal, a medal which, later in the century, was translated into the George Cross.

But the shade of Lieutenant Charles Herbert Collet of the Royal Marine Artillery and Royal Naval Air Service, flying a Sopwith three-seater Tractor Biplane with its 80 horsepower Gnome rotary engine, may claim to have conducted the first ever strategic bombing raid in history.

A number of the early naval bomber pilots transferred into the new Royal Air Force in 1918 and eventually achieved high rank. The career of Major Eugene Gerrard of the Royal Marine Light Infantry survived the destruction of his planes on the sand dunes of Ostend. One of the first four naval officers who had learned to fly in 1911 and who had accompanied Charles Collet on his epoch-making raid, Gerrard went on to win the Distinguished Service Order and, in due course, to become an air commodore in the Royal Air Force. Reggie Marix, who destroyed the Zeppelin in the shed at Düsseldorf, lost a leg in an air crash but carved out a career on the ground and died in 1966 an air vice-marshal. Charles Edmonds also became an air vice-marshal and served in the Second World War in that rank. John Babington became an air chief marshal and commanded Britain's air force in the Far East shortly before the Second World War. It was very clear to him that the British forces in that theatre were gravely ill prepared and he worked tirelessly to try and improve the readiness of his command for war. To the day he died in 1979, he regretted that he had not been able to do more to improve the situation before war engulfed the region. After a family dispute, he changed his name to Tremayne, his mother's maiden name.

Ferdinand von Zeppelin had died in 1917 but mention of his name was to invoke awe and foreboding in Britain right through the First World War. Even today, the machines he sired and the sense of menace they engendered are remembered, and the concept still has the power to intrigue. From time to time rigid airships stage a comeback and with increasing concerns about the environmental effects of large aircraft, it is by no means certain that we have heard the last of them.

It was not only the Royal Navy that was shaped by the existence of the Zeppelin. Sole possession of Zeppelins meant that the Germans did not have to counter them as a threat, and this played its part in shaping the Imperial High Sea Fleet. The chief German aviation requirement was for long-range scouting aircraft in the North Sea. The Zeppelin performed this function admirably, saving the High Seas Fleet's bacon when it came out again after Jutland and narrowly escaped being cut off by the Grand Fleet. Zeppelins also shared with seaplanes the burden of patrolling and protecting the coastal littoral between the Netherlands and Denmark, and in the Baltic. However, starting from small beginnings, Germany also very quickly built up a very useful German Naval Air Service of which the Naval Airship Division was only one part.

For the German Navy, there was not the same impetus to develop the combat aircraft carrier capable of operating seamlessly with a seagoing fleet, but that did not stop the Germans from conducting trials with some very innovative concepts to extend the range of their aircraft. While Commodore Tyrwhitt was planning a second attack on Cuxhaven in January 1915, the commander of the German base at Zeebrugge was seeking to extend the radius of a seaplane by piggy-backing it on to a submarine. The experiment was successful insofar as the submarine took the plane to within range of the Kent coast where it flew undetected before returning to Zeebrugge. However, this combination was even more vulnerable and weather dependent than the early British seaplane carriers and the project was eventually abandoned. A number of German seaplane carriers was also converted from merchant ships, although none was fast enough to operate on the high seas in conjunction with front-line warships. They nevertheless performed important service in the Baltic, supporting seaplane operations against the Russians. This included developing and using torpedo bombers on operations against Russian ships and supporting a brilliant amphibious operation to secure the islands at the entrance to the Gulf of Riga.

After initial dependence on foreign aircraft, the German Naval Air Service developed and built a portfolio of seaplanes, many of which were built in Friedrichshafen and named for that town. Their pilots were active, able and aggressive, and there were some outstanding flyers among them. It was to the German Navy that went the prize of being the first to inflict total destruction of a surface fleet at sea from the air. On 11 August 1918, a squadron of six British motor torpedo boats in the Heligoland Bight was attacked by seaplanes. None returned. Three were rendered immobile and drifted to the neutral Netherlands where they were interned; the other three were sunk. The British had paid the penalty for playing around in Germany's back yard once too often.

When Germany started building warships again in the 1930s, Versailles Treaty constraints meant that she started with vessels that nominally came within the terms of that treaty. Thus, in 1929, she built the so-called pocket battleships *Lützow*, *Scheer* and *Graf Spee*. In 1935, she laid down the battleships *Scharnhorst* and *Gneisenau*, and in 1936 she got round to building through-deck, fast, combat aircraft carriers. Two hulls of 19,000 tons were laid down. They were to carry forty aircraft each and be capable of 32 knots, and they would undoubtedly have been impressive, powerful ships. The first one was launched at Kiel in December 1938 and reached an advanced state of construction but, in April 1940, resources were diverted from her to the U-boat building programme. The second hull was abandoned and scrapped on the stocks.[5] Only when the Pacific War broke out, and the role of carriers in the destruction of the new battleship Bismark became clear, did Hitler resume construction of the first hull, and the conversion of other ships. None was ever completed. But, how appropriate it was that the first of these two fine ships was to be called the *Graf Zeppelin*, and the second one the *Peter Strasser*.

And as for Herbert George Wells, whose science fiction novel *The War in the Air* excited so much interest in 1908, he died in his bed in 1946 and quite clearly felt that he had been vindicated by all that had happened in between times. In his preface to the 1941 edition of his 1908 work, he declared that his epitaph should be: 'I told you so. You *damned* fools.'[6]

Notes

1 Soames, Mary, *Clementine Churchill*, Cassell, 1979, pp. 99-102.

2 Jenkins, Roy, *Churchill*, Pan Books, 2002, p. 349.

3 Ibid., p. 349.

4 Strachan, Hew (selected by), *Military Lives*, OUP, 2002, p. 450.

5 *Jane's Fighting Ships of World War II*, Studio Editions, 1990, p. 146.

6 Wells, Herbert G., *The War in the Air*, Penguin Classics, 2005, p. 279.

Bibliography

Ballantyne, Iain, *Warspite: Warships of the Royal Navy*, Leo Cooper, 2001.

Bennett, Geoffrey, *Coronel and the Falklands*, Birlinn Ltd, 2000.

Best, Geoffrey, *Churchill: A Study in Greatness*, Penguin, 2002.

Bleibler, Jürgen, *Luftkrieg über Friedrichshafen 1914-1918*, Wissenschaftliches Jahrbuch 2001, Zeppelin Museum, Friedrichsafen.

Burt, R.A., *British Battleships of World War One*, Arms and Armour Press, 1986.

Churchill, Winston, *The World Crisis 1911-1914*, Thornton Butterworth, 1923.

——, *The World Crisis 1915*, Charles Scribner's Sons, 1929.

Clark, Wesley, *Waging Modern War*, Public Affairs, 2001.

Cooper, Bryan and John Batchelor, 'Bombers 1914-1919', Purnell's History of the World Wars, BPC Publishing Ltd.

Craig, Gordon, *Germany 1866-1945*, OUP, 1978.

Creagh, Sir O'Moore and Humphris E.M., *The VC and the DSO*, vol. II, Standard Book Club, 1920.

Forder, Nick, 'The Friedrichshafen Raid', *WW I Aero Magazine*, May 1990.

Gordon, Andrew, *The Rules of the Game: Jutland and British Naval Command*, John Murray, 1996.

Haslam, E.B., *The History of Royal Air Force Cranwell*, HMSO, 1982.

Holmes, Gerard, *Christmas 1914*, privately published, 1920

Holmes, Richard, *In the Footsteps of Churchill*, BBC Books, 2005.

Howarth, David *Sovereign of the Seas: The Story of British Sea Power*, Book Club Associates, 1974.

Jane's Fighting Ships of World War I, Studio Editions, 1990.

Jane's Fighting Ships of World War II, Studio Editions, 1990.

Jenkins, Roy, *Churchill*, Pan Books, 2002.

Jones, H.A., *Official History of the War: The War in the Air*, vol II, OUP, 1929.

Jones, Neville, *The Origins of Strategic Bombing*, William Kimber, 1973.

King, Brad, *Royal Naval Air Service 1914-1918*, Hikoki Publications, 1997.

Kennet, Lee, *The First Air War 1914-1918*, Simon & Schuster, 1999.

Kershaw, Andrew (ed.), *Purnell's History of the World Wars: The First War Planes*, BPC Publishing, 1975.

Layman, R.D., *Naval Aviation in the First World War*, Chatham Publishing, 1996.

——, *The Cuxhaven Raid: The World's First Carrier Air Strike*, Conway Maritime Press, 1985.

Lea, John, *Reggie: The Life of Air Marshal R.L.G. Marix CBE DSO*, Pentland Press, 1994.

Levine, Joshua, *On a Wing and a Prayer*, HarperCollins, 2008.

Liddell Hart, Basil, *History of the First World War*, Book Club Associates in arrangement with Cassell & Co, 1970.

Lovering T.T.A. (ed.), *Ambhibious Assault: Manoevre from the Sea*, Crown Copyright, 1995.

London Gazette, 19 February 1915.

Lucas, John, *The Big Umbrella: The History of the Parachute*, Elm Tree Books, 1973.

Norman, Aaron, *The Great Air War: The Men, The Planes, The Saga of Military Aviation, 1914-1918*, Macmillan, 1968.

Raleigh, Walter, *Official History of the War: the War in the Air Vol I.*, OUP, 1939.

Rennles , Keith, *Independent Force: The War Diary of the Daylight Squadrons of the Independent Air Force, June–November 1918*, Grub Street, 2002,

Rimmel, Raymond, *Zeppelin! A Battle for Air Supremacy in World War One*, Conway Maritime Press, 1984.

Robinson, Douglas, *The Zeppelin in Combat*, Foulis & Co, 1971.

Royle, Trevor, *The Flowers of the Forest: Scotland and the First World War*, Birlinn, 2008.

Samson, Charles, *Fights and Flights*, Ernest Benn Ltd, 1930.

Sheffield, Gary, *Forgotten Victory. The First World War: Myths and Realities*, Headline Publishing, 2001.

Soames, Mary, *Clementine Churchill*, Cassell, 1979.

Steel, Nigel and Hart, Peter, *Tumult in the Clouds: The British Experience of the War in the Air, 1914-1918*, Hodder and Stoughton, 1997.

Strachan, Hew (selected by), *Military Lives*, OUP, 2002.

Stoney, Barbara, *Twentieth Century Maverick: The Life of Noel Pemberton Billing*, Bank House Books, 2004.

Sturtivant, Ray and Page, Gordon, *Royal Navy Aircraft Serials and Units 1911 to 1919*, Tonbridge: Air-Britain Historians, 1992.

Sueter, Murray, *Airman or Noahs*, Pitman and Sons, 1928.

Sueter, Murray, *The Evolution of the Tank*, Hutchinson, 1937.

Thompson, Julian, *The Imperial War Museum Book of the War at Sea 1914-1918*, Pan Books, 2005.

Treadwell, Terry, *The First Naval Air War*, Tempus Publishing Ltd, 2002.

Turner, Charles, *The Old Flying Days*, Ayer Publishing, 1972.

Wells, Herbert G, *The War in the Air*, Penguin Classics, 2005.

Wood, Eric, *Thrilling Deeds of British Airmen*, Harrap, 1917.

UNPUBLISHED PAPERS

Babington, John, 'A 1914 Naval Air Affair', from the papers of Mrs Penelope Willis, 1962, edited by Dr Norman Lyne.

Cabinet Office Paper CAB 37/121/123, at Public Record Office, Kew.

Gudehus, H.C. Gustav, 'Persönliche Erinnerungen' (aufgezeichnet von ihm selbst i.d. 1934) ['Personal memoirs' (recorded by himself in 1934)] from the papers of Dr Timm Gudehus, Blankenese, Hamburg, Germany.

Royal Naval Air Service Operational Reports ADM 116/1352 at Public Record Office, Kew.

Zeppelin Museum Archives, Paper LZA 3/6, Tagesbericht vom Samstag, den 21.November 1914.

Index

hands over responsibility for air defence of UK to Navy, 38-9

takes back responsibility for air defence of UK, 107

British government

attitude to parachutes, 30-1

failure to constitute an 'air board' for Royal Flying Corps, 20

forms Royal Air Force, 132

forms Royal Flying Corps, 1, 17-18

offered patents for flight by Wright brothers, 16

policy on Royal Flying Corps distorted, 16

policy towards developments in aerial navigation, 14-16

sends Churchill to Antwerp, 54

Brock, Lieutenant Frank, 61-2, 64

Budds, Chief Petty Officer Gilbert, 101, 104, 110

Buller, General Sir Redvers, 57

C

Calthrop, Mr Everard, 30

Cannon, Flight Sub Lieutenant Roland, 59, 60-1, 70-1, 80

Central Flying School, 17, 20

Chadwick, Mr Roy, 60

Childers, Lieutenant Erskine, 4, 91-2, 100, 103-4, 110

Churchill, Mr Winston

advice to Swiss government, 83

at Antwerp, 47-8, 54

becomes Secretary for War and Air, 135

concerns about Zeppelins, 39-40

departure from Admiralty, 107, 139

depression with war news, 56-7

First Lord of the Admiralty, 2, 24

gives permission for Düsseldorf Raid from lavatory, 47-8

influence on Royal Naval Air Service, 2, 19-20, 24-5, 38, 131

intention to strike Zeppelins in their bases, 39-40

orders acquisition of Sopwith Tabloids, 46-7

orders Cuxhaven Raid, 86

orders Friedrichshafen Raid, 57

part in invention of tank, 41

personality, 24

praise for first bomber pilots, 110

proposals to deal with Zeppelins, 25

reaction to Admiral Fisher's concerns about Zeppelins, 39

H

Halahan, Lieutenant Commander, 101-2

Hales

bombs, 44, 48, 60, 74, 89

grenades, 33

Harris, Marshal of the Royal Air Force Lord Arthur, 29-30

Harwich Force, *see* Tyrwhitt, Reginald

heavier-than-air flight, 12-13, 15-17, 24, 33, 110, 131

Heligoland, 11, 88, 93, 95, 97, 99-102, 104, 110

battle, 53, 55, 85, 87, 113

Henderson, Captain Ian, 140-1

Henderson, Major General Sir David, *see also* Trenchard *and* Sykes, 135, 140-1

assisted Smuts in forming Royal Air Force, 132-3

belief in reconnaissance role for aircraft, 19-20, 131

'father of the Royal Air Force', 19

resigns, 133

vice president of Air Council, 133

Hewlett, Flight Commander Francis, 102, 110

High Seas Fleet of Imperial German Navy, *see also* Admiral Scheer, 37, 55-6, 127

Admiral Tirpitz's view of

Zeppelins regarding, 14

at Jutland, 113-15

battleship race with Royal Navy, 11-13

British attempts to lure out of base, 88-9, 104

failure to use Zeppelins to full potential, 113, 118

saved by Zeppelins, 93

Hipper, Admiral Franz von, 114-15

Hogg, Major, 141

I

Immelmann, Oberleutnant Max, 4

Imperial German Navy, *see also* High Seas Fleet, 22, 23, 38, 53

attitude to parachutes, 125

attitude to Zeppelins, 14, 16, 27, 112

procures first Zeppelin, 14

strategy, 11-12

Independent Force, 133-4

J

Jackson, Admiral Sir Henry, 9

Jellicoe, Admiral Sir John

experience with *Campania*, 108, 114

part in Cuxhaven Raid, 87-9

part in Jutland battle, 113-15

points out impotence against scouting Zeppelins, 110

air committee, 18

aircraft procurement policy, 20, 46-7

deploys to war, 36-7

disregard of Zeppelins, 20

failure to constitute an 'air board', 20

focused on tactical support of Army, 20, 130

formation, 17-18

ill-equipped for bombing, 130

limited bombing capability, 32-3

Military Wing, 1, 18-20, 29

concept of mutual support with Naval Wing, 18

Naval Wing, 1

concept of mutual support with Military Wing, 18

evolution into Royal Naval Air Service, 2, 20

formation, 17-18

preoccupation with reconnaissance, 1, 20, 24-5, 130

responsible for air defence of UK, 26, 38,

Zeppelin the stimulus for parentage, 19-20, 112

Royal Marine Artillery, 6, 44, 142

Royal Marine Light Infantry, 17, 42, 44, 92, 142

Royal Marines, 2, 19, 38, 44, 141

Royal Naval Air Service, *see also* Royal Flying Corps, Royal Air Force and Royal Navy, 1-4, 11,19, 23-4, 46-7, 54, 139-40

divergent approach from Royal Flying Corps, 131

Churchill's influence, 2, 6, 24-5, 39-40, 130-1, 139

conduct of Cuxhaven Raid, 88-105

conduct of first Düsseldorf Raid, 44

conduct of second Düsseldorf Raid, 45-50

conduct of Friedrichshafen Raid, 57-81

deploys to war, 37-8

development of radios, 33

evolution from Naval Wing, 20

invention of armoured cars, 40-2

land operations in Belgium, 40-2

true precursors of Royal Air Force, 4

preoccupied with Zeppelins, 33

state at outbreak of war, 33

strategic bombing of Germany from France, 131

styles of rank, 2-3

takes responsibility for air defence of UK, 38-9